SIMON CALLOW

Simon Callow is an actor on stage, film and television, a director of plays, operas and musicals, and a writer and translator.

For the National, during Peter Hall's directorate, he played Orlando in *As You Like It*, Stafford in *Sisterly Feelings*, the title role in *Amadeus*, the Little Monk in *The Life of Galileo* and performed Shakespeare's complete Sonnets as a Platform performance. During Richard Eyre's time as Director, in the double bill *Single Spies*, he appeared in both plays (as Guy Burgess in *An Englishman Abroad* and as Chubb in *A Question of Attribution* which he also directed). Most recently he was Face in *The Alchemist*. Previously, when Laurence Olivier was Director, he had worked on the bookstall, been an usher and a member of the box office staff.

His books include: *Being An Actor, Shooting the Actor, Acting in Restoration Comedy*, translations of Cocteau's *The Infernal Machine* and Milan Kundera's *Jacques and his Master*, and biographies of Charles Laughton *(A Difficult Actor)*, and Orson Welles *(The Road to Xanadu)*. His memoir of Peggy Ramsay will be published in Spring 1998.

Simon Callow

The National
The Theatre and its Work
1963-1997

with a Preface by
Trevor Nunn

contributions from
Richard Findlater
Richard Eyre
Peter Hall
and members of the National's audience

and a
Chronology of Productions
1963-1997

NICK HERN BOOKS
London
in association with
ROYAL NATIONAL THEATRE
London

The National first published in Great Britain in 1997 in simultaneous hardback and paperback editions by Nick Hern Books Limited, 14 Larden Road, London W3 7ST in association with the Royal National Theatre, South Bank, London SE1 9PX

ISBN 1 85459 318 8 (Hardback)
1 85459 323 4 (Paperback)

A CIP catalogue record for this book is available from the British Library

Edited by **Lyn Haill**
Designed by **Michael Mayhew**

Printed and bound in Great Britain by Mackays of Chatham
Set in Plantin & Franklin Gothic

Contents

ACKNOWLEDGMENTS

Thanks to

Jack Bradley, John Carnegie, Richard Eyre, Peter Hall, Angela Findlater, John Goodwin, John Langley, Sue MacGregor, Richard Mangan, Trevor Nunn, Janet Prowting, Toby Radford, Nicola Scadding of the National's Archive, Sue Winter, Nicholas Wright, all the photographers whose work appears in these pages, and all the members of the National's audience who sent in recollections of performances at and impressions of the Theatre, some of which are included with photographs in the chronology section

Books quoted or consulted by Simon Callow include: *The History of the National Theatre* by Nicholas Tomalin and John Elsom (Jonathan Cape, 1978); *The National, A Dream Made Concrete* by Peter Lewis (Methuen, 1990); *Britain's Royal National Theatre, the first 25 years* by Tim Goodwin (National Theatre and Nick Hern Books, 1988); *Confessions of an Actor* (1982) and *On Acting* by Laurence Olivier (1986); *Peter Hall's Diaries* (ed. John Goodwin, Hamish Hamilton, 1984) *Making An Exhibition of Myself* by Peter Hall (Sinclair Stevenson, 1994), *The Life of Kenneth Tynan* by Kathleen Tynan (1987), *The Letters of Kenneth Tynan* (ed. Kathleen Tynan, 1994), *The British Theatre* by Peter Noble (1946)

Front cover: Photograph by Peter Cook

Back cover: Photograph of Laurence Olivier and Peter Hall (Hulton Picture Library) Photograph of Trevor Nunn and Richard Eyre by John Haynes

Introduction
by Trevor Nunn

I suppose premonition is the nearest idea we itemise in our language as the opposite to "déjà vu" and it's something like that, the unnerving sense that the future will be entirely familiar, which I have been feeling while reading this tightly compacted essay on the brief and brilliant history of the National Theatre.

Partly because I have run a continually threatened, state subsidized arts organization for nearly two decades, and partly because I have personally known the protagonist cast of this book, sharing many a meal and confidence with them over the years, this history of financial crisis, ceaseless repertoire demand and enforced compromise seems to me an eerily recognizable landscape in which I have dwelt long; even at times it is mistakable for the terrain of my autobiography.

The gift of foreknowledge, as we know from Merlin onwards, can also be a curse, and it would be entirely wrong of me to assume that the rough scree and sheer inclines up which the National Theatre must struggle over the next few years will have any of the characteristics of the mountains that have been scaled by the three great expedition leaders whose achievements here read like an adventure story in the heroic tradition.

I used to visit Laurence Olivier in his hut in Aquinas Street (like Timon of Athens receiving embassies from the outside world) and even though we were there to discuss potential conflicts of repertoire between our two organizations in a relationship of theoretical parity, I was never anything but in awe of him. Each meeting was like being in an anecdote; especially on the winter night when the power failed and I sat opposite him in a space no bigger than a railway compartment, the laconic expressions of his world- famous face illuminated by a small hurricane lamp, the solitary sound of our talk late into the evening intensified by the "pouring dark". Indeed I thought of Henry V and war-time that night. For whatever reason the National was unable to plan as far ahead as the schemes I was outlining with prepared confidence. Larry chuckled and swore with Churchillian relish and then, more quietly, he said "You youngsters ... I tell you, this isn't a game you want to be too old for".

The phrase "punishing schedule" and variations recur during the ensuing pages rather a lot, like a muted motif on the timpani, behind or between glorious flourishes from the brass. As evidenced in his diaries, I witnessed a good deal of Peter Hall's schedule at the NT and thought its punishments positively masochistic. But at the RSC, Peter had already provided us with the nation's first large-scale theatre ensemble working in repertoire, followed by working in repertoire in two theatres a hundred miles apart, which, like Roger Bannister running a sub-four minute mile, seemed to be impossible before he did it. So, unfairly perhaps, the yet more death-defying feat of scheduling and running three contrasting auditoriums – plus a host of ancillary activities – towards the expression of a coherent policy of which one vital component had to be box office success, was something the press and the public alike expected Peter to be able to bring off. You've broken four minutes, so of course you can break three.

His achievement was no less than the sine qua non of the National as we know it, and the cost to him in human terms impossible any longer to quantify. Like any hero returned from a mission impossible, he will say "Oh, it was nothing" but I would bet there were any number of times when Peter, with all his experience, felt very alone and more than a bit afraid.

I have had a rare and privileged opportunity to observe at close quarters exactly how the impossible job is done by occupying the room next door to Richard Eyre's office for nine months, with the connecting door wide open for much of the time; it is as if I have been watching a fly-on-the-wall television documentary without any of that iniquitous selective editing to distort or over-simplify.

Having known him since we were both teenagers, I suppose I was to some extent tickled by the thought of Richard, who had once been so irreverent and rebellious, now become an authority figure, something like Vaclav Havel becoming President. But soon I discovered there was no longer any amusement in my findings because my amazement left me no room for anything else. However hard I try I have never once managed to get to the National Theatre building before him; perhaps suffering from insomnia should be part of the job description and perhaps, like all Shakespeare's troubled leaders who wish the finger hadn't pointed to them, uneasy will always lie the head that runs the NT. Often working late myself, I have invariably discovered the only other office not yet locked and given over to security staff is Richard's, who is hosting a sponsorship evening or speaking to a group of international directors, or remaining on duty because a government minister has come to see a show.

Peter Brook once mischievously observed to me that the biggest acting ensemble I should set up would consist of twenty-three actors. When I questioned his selection of this apparently random number, he said it was because each actor would need an hour a day of the artistic director's time, and "it would be good to have an hour for yourself". I have been watching Richard attend to the needs of three acting companies simultaneously, three groups of technical staff, an unprecedentedly demanding fund-raising campaign, the beginnings of the crucial refurbishment work which he initiated, while directing a sequence of immensely varied and equally successful productions almost without a break between one and the next, and I think the mot juste to describe my reaction is "boggled".

Like watching those extraordinary conjurors who entertain at your table in a restaurant, I have been so close up to the trick I feel I must be able to work out how it is done (especially since I used to be a member of the Circle) but I can't. It's magic.

Theatre is of course a communal achievement and the number of things that must cohere to make something extraordinary happen is influenced by luck as well as judgement. Very bold planning intentions get derailed by the equivalent of leaves on the track, and it is unwise to advertise new policy targets when the smallest jiggle can cause you to miss the board altogether. That is why theatre historians have twenty-twenty hindsight, and theatre directors develop a knack of describing past happenstance as evidence of their clear philosophic intentions.

However, I am much moved to discover in Dick Findlater's account of the history of the National Theatre building, the six point declaration of the aims of a National Theatre presented in a hand-book published in 1909. I would be very happy for this list to be nailed to the doors of the NT back and front, pre- and post-refurbishment, especially if I could add in manuscript that these aims should never smack of exclusivity or privilege but be for the benefit of everybody of whatever background regionally, racially, religiously and not forgetting children, whose needs should be close to the heart of the National's aspirations.

A history like this is bound to be partial and personal and the subjects may well offer different accounts when or if they choose to commit themselves to print. But the real history is in the imaginations and inspirations of those individuals, thousands or even millions of them, who came, who saw and were conquered, or more precisely were changed, in ways to which the fashionable detractors of the theatre are sadly not open. The facts and the critical consensus have no bearing on such a history because it is the history of impressions as ephemeral as the movement of light. Whatever dispute might amuse the participants as their memories vie with these pages, nothing can change what is celebrated here, as Gerard Manley Hopkins said with his matchless enthusiasm –

"– the achieve of, the mastery of the thing!"

August 1997

The First Thirty-five Years
by Simon Callow

In contemplating the brief history of Britain's National Theatre, it is extraordinary to realise the degree to which its birth and subsequent short life have been fraught with difficulty and surrounded with conflict – extraordinary because the theatre (and the drama, insofar as they are separable things) have been since the first Elizabethan era among the conspicuous successes of British culture, earning for themselves a pre-eminence in that area scarcely challenged by any other nation. And yet the theatre in this country has always been a source of contention, feared and harassed by the political establishment (to the point of being altogether banned for the years of the Cromwellian Commonwealth and vigorously censored from the middle of the eighteenth century to beyond the middle of the twentieth). It has had to fight and to fight hard to achieve even a bare level of respectability, let alone the enthusiastic endorsement and rich public subsidy of every other European nation. This division from the state has not been all loss, of course, partly accounting for the theatre's exceptional liveliness and its ability to exist at an angle to the prevailing values of the day. But from the middle of the last century, with the increasing cost and sophistication of productions, and with the development of exceptional ensembles in Europe and Russia, it had become glaringly evident that for the theatre to advance, or even to maintain its levels of excellence, some sort of public subsidy, and for that matter, public endorsement, was essential. The history of the idea of a national theatre in Britain, from its conception to its birth after a gestation of over a hundred years, is told elsewhere in this book; but it is a necessary background to the thirty-five-year-old history of the National Theatre as it finally came into existence, and to the régimes of the three men who have run the company during that time. In retrospect, their three artistic directorships seem to have very clear-cut and separate identities, which, given the unceasing struggle to survive, even to exist, it is hardly fanciful to describe in epic terms.

Laurence Olivier:
Founding Father

It was touch-and-go till the very last moment. The parliamentary Bill which provided a million post-war pounds for the establishment and endowment of a National Theatre had remained passively on the statutes since its enactment in 1949, cynically unimplemented despite the Royal unveiling of a foundation stone on the South Bank and a growing rage from the theatrical profession which united critics, writers, directors and actors of every shade: "the spiritual life of the nation is at stake!" roared even Donald Wolfit, the man most unlikely to be invited to be a member of any possible National Theatre. The Labour-controlled London County Council finally forced the Conservative government's hand in 1960, by offering a million pounds in matching funds to create what was originally planned to be a huge complex including both theatre and opera house, erected to the greater glory of the capital and the nation. The government could refuse no longer, and the long tease was over.

The immediate task was the appointment of an artistic director. Who would have the clout, the energy and the experience to organise and lead the great enterprise? In retrospect, there was really only ever one answer: Laurence Olivier – partly because he wanted it so much, mostly because of his commanding position within the profession, and scarcely less important than either of these because of the powerful campaign which had been waged on his behalf for nearly seven years by one of the most formidable political operators of his time, Oliver Lyttelton, Viscount Chandos, who had earned his place in history as Churchill's wartime Minister of Supplies (and thus Albert Speer's opposite number), and who wanted to seal his reputation by finally establishing Britain's National Theatre. "What we want from you is a glamourpuss," he told Olivier, which is certainly what they got, and in overplus. But they got something considerably more. No other actor in Britain could have brought to the job what he did: theatre star, movie star, theatre director, movie director, West End producer, commanding in the classical repertory and triumphant in the commercial theatre, as well as bold champion – in marked contrast to the nervous rest of his generation – of the avant-garde: Ionesco, Osborne and David Turner. He had even married, in a manner of speaking, into the Royal Court, his relationship with Joan Plowright symbolically sealing his position at the meeting point of the old and the new.

If the artistic director of the National Theatre was to be an actor, Olivier must be that actor. There was, however, a widespread feeling, especially in circles of influence, that the time of the actor-manager was over. In fact, some years before, the brilliant if idiosyncratic director Tyrone Guthrie had been privately approached to head the National by an influential group which included Peter Hall and Kenneth Tynan, but he publicly disavowed any desire to be involved. As it happens, it was Guthrie, a sometimes mischievous figure hovering in the wings, who had been instrumental, some fifteen years earlier, in securing the dismissal from the directorship of the Old Vic of the world-beating team of Olivier, Ralph Richardson and the director John Burrell, on the grounds that if the Old Vic were being groomed for transformation into a National Theatre, only a director could adequately head the company. By a small irony of history, it was in fact those legendary seasons at the New Theatre when the Old Vic company had been bombed out of its own building, that were very clearly the inspiration for the early seasons of the National when it was finally established. That sequence of astonishing productions at the New – *Cyrano de Bergerac, Henry IV, Peer Gynt, Oedipus* and *King Lear* – had scaled unprecedented heights of theatrical excellence, creating a new, uniquely urgent, relationship with the audience, and it was that wartime spirit, with its attendant sense of renewal, that was to be the prevailing atmosphere of the early years of the National Theatre at the Old Vic.

In 1946, Olivier, oblivious of the dismissal that was at any moment about to be served on him, had written: "The Old Vic has for some time been, in people's minds, the National Theatre; it is now destined to be in fact. We have had much talk of a National Theatre in the past, but it should be realised that such a venture requires considerably more than the mere building components. The edifice itself is important, but this is as nothing compared with the people who are to be concerned with operating such a theatre. It is the human raw material which matters most – the administrators, directors, playwrights, actors, stage managers, designers, painters, technicians, and musicians …may we also hope that the thousands of new audiences who have been attracted to stage plays in the past few years will continue to take pleasure in the great dramatic masterpieces of all time. But we must not forget new plays…we must encourage writers to work in the theatre medium; and in this respect I should like to see special playwrights' schools attached to theatres in much the same way that some theatres possess dramatic academies for their acting students…let us hope that the rebirth of our theatre, both in

Laurence Olivier
(Photo: Zoë Dominic)

the intrinsic artistic sense and in the fact of the general increase of interest in worthwhile plays, will be a feature of post-war Britain. For a nation which loves its theatre is a healthy nation."

Since writing those words, Olivier had dreamed of nothing but creating the National Theatre. For a man to such a large degree fuelled by the need to prove himself superior to all competition, and somehow to assure for himself a position, not merely distinguished but unassailable, in the annals of theatrical history, it was an obvious dream: his personal glory and that of the organisation fused. Charles Laughton had said to him after seeing his Henry V in 1937: "Larry, you know why you're so good in this? It's because when you play Henry, you *are* England." Now he would *be* the National Theatre. He went about it with passion and shrewdness and discipline. As a sort of dress rehearsal for the grander job, he accepted the directorship of the newly-built Chichester Festival Theatre shortly before his appointment to the directorship of the National Theatre was announced. The opening season at Chichester was accordingly closely scrutinised, by no-one more keenly than his greatest and most articulate fan, the critic Kenneth Tynan, for whom he was and always had been the very model of what great acting should be. Tynan was nonetheless fiercely critical of the first two plays chosen, with the manner of their presentation – *The Chances* and *The Broken Heart*, both obscure, both awkwardly staged by Olivier himself – and even with the performances, Olivier's included. With characteristic chutzpah he wrote to Olivier after *The Broken Heart*, enclosing his damning review in case it had escaped Olivier's attention, and asked to be appointed Literary Manager. Astonishingly, but also entirely characteristically, Olivier took him on, candidly admitting that he wanted to silence a potentially dangerous voice ("Anything to get you off that *Observer*!"), but also believing, quite correctly, that Tynan had his finger on the pulse of what was theatrically current. Olivier was always haunted by the fear of being left behind by theatrical fashion; with Tynan at his side he could be sure that that never happened. He would, moreover, Olivier felt, add intellectual weight to the organisation. In fact, brilliance rather than weight was what Tynan had to offer, that and a range and speed of sympathies that was stimulating and imaginative; he would keep Olivier on his toes. The great actor laboured all his life under a painful intellectual inferiority complex, and was almost too eager to listen to the advice of others in matters of intellectual judgement. The influence that Tynan came to exercise over him was considerable, to the rage of many people, both outside the organisation and within it, who were darkly suspicious of what John Osborne called Tynan's "intellectual spivvery".

The partnership between these two extraordinary and ill-assorted men, the greatest actor of his day and the greatest critic, constituted a relationship which was uncommon and indeed – in the English theatre at any rate – unprecedented. William Archer and Harley Granville Barker, in *A Scheme and Estimates for a National Theatre*, had proposed that its leadership should ideally be in the hands of two people, an artistic director and a literary manager; but Tynan's input went considerably beyond what they had envisaged, beyond even that of a European *dramaturg*, the job on which Tynan's was modelled. His contribution started, in fact, with the company. Tynan took an active interest in scheduling, in the composition of the company and in its overall development, matters which he rightly felt to have a direct bearing on the repertory and its performance. It was Tynan rather than Olivier who articulated their ambitions for the company, even before the operation had begun: it was to be an ensemble flexible enough to perform the whole range of world drama, adapting its style to the requirements of each play rather than

Top: Harley Granville Barker

Below: Kenneth Tynan with Olivier

8

imposing one on it. Tynan's genius as a critic had been as a connoisseur of acting rather than as a judge of literature, so he was bound to be actively concerned about the acting of the new Company. In this he and Olivier were as one. Tynan had described his ideal in the celebrated phrase High Definition Performance: "supreme professional polish, hard-edged technical skill, the effortless precision without which no artistic enterprise can inscribe itself on our memory – the hypnotic saving grace of high and low art alike, the common denominator that unites tragedy, ballroom dancing, conversation and cricket." Asked to describe the sort of actors he wanted for his company, Olivier replied: "very good ones. Versatile ones; people with their hearts in the right place; unlazy ones, deeply enthusiastic, courageous, gifted with all sorts of attributes. The nature of their work demands physical – not perfection – but prowess."

They took as axiomatic the interdependence of the repertory and the company. Olivier had in mind a race of super-actors, a sort of theatrical SAS, daring and winning, able triumphantly to deal with any challenge thrown at them. Both men were hugely exercised by the question of the recruitment and development of the acting company. Intending to maintain, as they claimed, an extensive repertory – the "library" of 49 essential plays that Harley Granville Barker had prescribed as the minimum for a national company, some being scrapped every year to make room for new productions – they clearly had a substantial task on their hands. "There are two big problems in any company attempting as large a repertoire as the National Theatre eventually hopes to have," said Tynan in a slightly uneasy interview with Charles Marowitz in *Encore*. "One will be this question of period style...I should hate to have to cast *The Importance of Being Earnest* out of a cast of New Wave actors... The other problem...is the fact that there are very few solid actors of weight between say, forty and sixty...these actors, who are the backbone of the German theatre and the Russian theatre simply don't exist in England. We have our one or two great stars – but where are the people who are automatic casting for, say, Gloucester in *Lear*?" Unlike Peter Hall and his newly-created Royal Shakespeare Company (a mere three years older than the National), they had no house dramatist on whom to hone a style, nor an artistic director with a particular aesthetic. There was no theory, no method; everything was in the doing. "I don't think Larry had such a thing as an aesthetic," observed Peter Wood, one of the Company's first directors. "What attracted him were bloody good plays, wonderful theatrical situations – something to keep the audience awake at night...Larry had a real, almost a young man's idealistic dream about a National Theatre, peopled by the best actors in the world doing the best plays in the world." Olivier himself, asked what he wanted from the National Theatre, simply said: "to make the audience applaud."

He succeeded in this beyond his or anyone's wildest dreams for a not insignificant period of time. This was achieved, again typically, by a judiciously pluralistic approach. His and Tynan's yearning for a glamorous, sexy theatre (in his maiden speech to the House of Lords he had described the theatre in a remarkable phrase as "the first glamouriser of thought") was balanced by the close alliance he formed with the young bloods of the Royal Court – the directors John Dexter and William Gaskill, the actors Robert Stephens, Frank Finlay, Colin Blakely and Joan Plowright, and the designer Jocelyn Herbert, underpinned by an increased closeness to George Devine, the inspiration of them all. Their neo-Brechtian approach, bare and textured, supplemented by the radical social realism which was such a strong strand of their work, was a perfect counterpoint to Olivier's inclinations towards glamour. The acting company for the first

The Old Vic in the 60s

season was recruited from the broadest possible spectrum of available talent: classical actors (Michael Redgrave and Edith Evans), West End stars (the young Maggie Smith, for example, and the veteran Max Adrian), and raw, hungry young actors, many from the Royal Court (Robert Stephens, Frank Finlay, Colin Blakely, Ian McKellen). The reps were combed for the boldest and most colourful of young hopefuls, whose number included Derek Jacobi and Anthony Hopkins (Michael Gambon came from the amateur theatre), all carrying their proverbial spears, but not for long: the essential principle of building company strength from within was scrupulously maintained in those early days.

As if to confirm the continuity with Lilian Baylis's work and that of the Richardson-Olivier years, while the new building was being conceived and constructed, the National Theatre had its temporary home at the Old Vic, and it was from that famous and historic stage that on 22 October 1963, the Company, so ardently and for so long planned, the focus of so many hopes and dreams, had its somewhat muted official launch. Olivier's production of *Hamlet*, slow, solemn, long, might best be described as an example of what Ken Campbell has vividly described as "brochure theatre". Peter O'Toole, hot from *Lawrence of Arabia* and minus a large portion of the splendid nose with which he had led in so many remarkable stage performances in the previous decade, gave exactly twenty-one surprisingly underpowered performances of the title role, after which the production was never seen again. Business began in earnest with a season which consisted of *Saint Joan*, *Uncle Vanya* (both transferred from Olivier's first season at Chichester), *The Recruiting Officer*, *Hobson's Choice*, Max Frisch's *Andorra*, *Othello*, Beckett's *Play* and the *Philoctetes* of Sophocles in a double bill, and finally *The Master Builder* – a repertory containing a familiar Shaw play stripped of piety and brought up fresh and new by two stars of the Royal Court, Joan Plowright and the director John Dexter; a haunting production of the Chekhov boasting a central group of performances including Michael Redgrave's of the title role which will probably never be equalled; Bill Gaskill's reclamation of Farquhar's comedy in the light of Brecht's radical rediscovery of it, with Maggie Smith supreme as Silvia; an honourable revival of one of the glories of the Manchester School of playwriting; a new and disturbing Swiss play with Tom Courtenay in the leading rôle; an ambitious if ultimately unsuccessful pairing of plays by Beckett and Sophocles; and a noble attempt at Ibsen's middle-period masterpiece, again with Redgrave, which fell short of triumph for him, but was nonetheless a rich addition to the repertory.

The climax of the season, inevitably, was Olivier's assumption of the title role in *Othello*, directed by Dexter, designed by Jocelyn Herbert (a Royal Court team again), potently timed to open on the 400th anniversary of Shakespeare's birth, 23 April 1964. Controversial in the extreme, anything but safe or cosy, vocally astonishing, as a physical achievement matchless even by his own extraordinary standards, Olivier's performance at the centre of the young company confirmed the one-year-old National Theatre's claim to being judged by the highest international standards. Nowhere else in the world could a more completely realised performance than his have been seen. And this from a man who had within a year created a whole theatrical enterprise from scratch, directed two of its productions and played another great rôle, Astrov, with subtle mastery and moving power.

The effect on the company of his electric presence among them, leading, quite literally, from the front, was potent in the extreme. The confidence within the company, the dedication and the application, were palpable, and the feeling spread throughout the

Olivier as Othello, 1964
(Photo: Angus McBean)

organisation. The Old Vic could not begin to contain the large administration required for the organisation. On a bomb-site in Aquinas Street, round the corner from the theatre, Olivier ran his company from a Portakabin, appropriately bunker-like for an approach to running a theatre which was almost on a war-footing. Like the actor-manager he was, he was interested in everything, and took responsibility for everything. Surprisingly for a man whose entire life had been a triumph of the will, he was happy to take advice; it was not his way to surround himself with like-minded people, but to pit one voice against another, with himself as arbiter, *primus inter pares*. At the beginning, when he himself was in full vigour, this worked remarkably well; later, indecisiveness set in and he sometimes seemed to become a feather for each wind that blew. In particular, his relationship with the Board and its formidable chairman, Lord Chandos, became unhappy, and the surprising question was raised of who was in charge.

In the first few years, though, Olivier and his colleagues created a unique atmosphere in the venerable building, cradle of the modern British theatre, now adapted yet again, this time by Sean Kenny, who stripped away the remaining Victorian features from the proscenium, making it stark and rough, and focusing attention on the stage rather than on the auditorium. The face the theatre presented to the world was carefully planned. A strikingly modern typographic font – very Sixties – was employed on all documents and public signs; there was to be nothing fuddy-duddy, nothing Establishment, about the National Theatre. The front-of-house operation was slick and efficient, with ushers smartly uniformed and strictly disciplined under the almost military leadership of the House Manager, Rupert Rhymes. A little hole in the wall had been converted into a surprisingly well-stocked bookstall, where the National Theatre's sumptuous new programmes could also be bought. Every detail of the operation seemed to reflect the company's sense of self. Backstage, conditions were dismal: poky, overcrowded dressing-rooms, primitive storage facilities. With little wing-space and only limited flying capacity it was necessary to transport every set away from the theatre at the end of the show. Somehow, though, these constrictions were part of the spirit of the enterprise: the Battle of Britain feeling, in the knowledge that all this was only temporary – soon a magnificent new building would rise on the South Bank, into which Sir (as Olivier was universally known) would lead his band of heroes, the happy few, up the road, to occupy it in glory.

In the meantime he had made sure, like a good general, that at the very least his troops were well fed. A canteen was installed, with an excellent, properly temperamental chef, and a menu at more than competitive prices, which meant that somehow the whole company piled into that tiny space, and technicians and ushers and actors and designers and directors rubbed shoulders and shanks, squeezing together round the little tables, feeling that they were all part of the same enterprise. Sir himself was often in evidence, generally choosing to sit with the ushers or the box office staff, in his kindly bank-manager persona, taking an interest, trying valiantly and not entirely unsuccessfully to remember each one – a touch of Larry in the night. He had made a heroic effort to know the names of, at the very least, every single member of the acting company – which sometimes ran to over a hundred – assisted by photographs, taken through the list by Joan Plowright as if he were learning one of his great rôles. He was the beating heart of the company: when he faltered, so did it.

Strength and energy and sheer muscular tone were the *sine qua non* of what he wanted from his actors, and they were provided with movement classes under the great Swedish teacher Yat Malmgren, and voice classes under Kate Fleming, both endorsed by Olivier's

Main picture:
Olivier at the window of the National's Aquinas Street offices
(Photo: Keystone)

1963 productions, *top to bottom:*

Robert Lang, Joan Plowright and Max Adrian in *Saint Joan*

Michael Redgrave and Joan Plowright in *Uncle Vanya*

Peter O'Toole as Hamlet
(Photos: Angus McBean)

enthusiastic, not to say fiercely competitive, participation; Tynan's dream of an acting studio at the National Theatre – "constant practice in a sort of acting gym", he promised Charles Marowitz in *Encore* – never quite materialised, but there was a more conventional gymnasium, with bar-bells and weights, in the basement, run by the theatre's formidable housekeeper Harry Henderson, who, in another incarnation, would appear every evening in the foyer, barely contained within his bursting dinner jacket, to police the clamouring hordes beating down the doors of what almost immediately became the Mecca of every true believing theatre-goer. Sometimes they would sleep all night on the pavement to queue for the forty or so day seats; otherwise they had somehow got their hands on what for many seasons were the hottest tickets in town, via the mailing list which was operated on the strictly democratic basis of first received, first served. If you failed to get a ticket in this booking period, you had preference for the next; even then, you might not get a ticket. Sometimes people would apply four or five times, and end up, triumphantly, with a restricted view seat in the upper circle. During the opening of each booking period, the box office spread over the whole theatre, with small armies of temporary staff working from trestle tables set up in the front-of-house coffee bars, at Aquinas Street, in the small office above the foyer which had been Lilian Baylis's – even in the rehearsal rooms if they were not being used, though they usually were: space was at a premium for every activity.

Dress rehearsals were an opportunity for the whole organisation to see the work just before the public did, and they were often festive occasions. The sense of unstoppable triumph persisted for some while; international tours (*Othello* in Moscow; *Love for Love* actually opened there), plus an occasional regional one, swelled the ever-growing glory. New plays joined the repertory from the second year: *The Royal Hunt of the Sun* was the first, and it was everything that Olivier had dreamed of for his company – a virtuoso production (by John Dexter) in a dazzlingly bold design (by Michael Annals) of a darkly questioning play (by Peter Shaffer), cast in epic form, performed by a company at a peak of physical fitness headed by the actor that Olivier now appointed as his second-in-command, Robert Stephens. His Atahualpa was a performance at once consummately realised and fearlessly experimental – precisely the combination that Olivier himself embodied, though the performance itself owed nothing whatever to Sir's personal style; the company was not going to be a troupe of Olivier clones. They now began, at Tynan's urging (and in the teeth of opposition from Gaskill and Dexter), to invite foreign directors to work with them: Jacques Charon for *A Flea In Her Ear*, Zeffirelli for *Much Ado About Nothing*, a production of the utmost theatrical enchantment and matchless glamour, which was about as far from a purist view of Shakespeare as could be contrived. The text itself had been reworked by Robert Graves to eliminate obscurity, though Zeffirelli's decision to have Dogberry and his crew use Italian accents had introduced, to deliciously comic effect, whole new levels of confusion not envisaged by the author. The production was framed in a trellis spangled with coloured lights, attended by human statues which would uncannily wink at the end of a scene, underscored with Nino Rota's music, alternately sentimental and boisterous, and acted by a company that could only otherwise have been assembled in heaven: Albert Finney, Derek Jacobi, Ian McKellen as the two Princes and Claudio, Lynn Redgrave as Margaret, Frank Finlay as Dogberry, and among the sundry smaller rôles, Edward Petherbridge, Michael Byrne, Ronald Pickup, Michael York and Christopher Timothy, with, right at the centre, Maggie Smith and Robert Stephens as a Beatrice and Benedick palpably sexy, vivaciously stylish and,

Main picture:
Robert Stephens and Colin Blakely in *The Royal Hunt of the Sun*, 1964
(Photo: Angus McBean)

Top right: John Stride, Albert Finney and Geraldine McEwan in *A Flea In Her Ear*, 1966
(Photo: Zoë Dominic)

Below right: Albert Finney and Robert Stephens in *Much Ado About Nothing*, 1965
(Photo: Zoë Dominic)

ultimately, affectingly tender. The production represented the quintessence of the Tynan-Olivier axis within the National Theatre, and it was the antithesis of everything that the Dexter-Gaskill team aspired to. That Gaskill's production of *The Recruiting Officer*, pared down to its hard reality, could co-exist in a repertory with this *Much Ado About Nothing* alla Siciliana – and with the same great actress in the central role of both productions – is a clear indication of just how broad was the church of which Olivier was Supreme Pontiff. Even Gaskill's and Dexter's work was to some extent influenced by the hedonistic spirit of the National Theatre at the Old Vic; the company were, as Tynan later precisely observed, Cavaliers to the RSC's Roundheads. *Performance* was the central notion of both Laurence Olivier and Kenneth Tynan, which implied a certain level of campness – or at the very least of flourish.

Flourish, oddly enough, was the name of the Royal Shakespeare Company's magazine, but the RSC's values were very different; in fact, each company's work at this time was largely defined in relation to the other. Paradoxically, the National Theatre was deeply influenced in its repertory and, often, in its choice of director, by an event sponsored by the RSC, the annual World Theatre Season at the Aldwych Theatre. This influence was perhaps inevitable, given the National's ideal of an *international* company, but productions like Jacques Charon's *A Flea In Her Ear*, *Hedda Gabler* (directed for the National Theatre, as at the World Theatre Season, by Ingmar Bergman), *The Architect and the Emperor of Assyria* (directed by Victor García, who had had extraordinary triumphs with Nuria Espert at the Aldwych) and *Saturday, Sunday, Monday* (Eduardo de Filippo and his company had brought *Napoli Milionaria*) were all direct spin-offs from those seasons so gallantly created by the legendary one-armed impresario Peter Daubeny, as was the use of designers like Josef Svoboda and Piero Gherardi. It was ironic that the RSC, squarely based on the Shakespearean canon, should have been, in feeling and in repertory, the more *national* of the two companies, more British in tone and texture than Olivier's flamboyantly vivacious, thoroughly eclectic outfit.

It is a measure of its strength as an ensemble that it had been perfectly possible for Tynan to commission Peter Shaffer to write a play, and to announce that play before a word had been written, confident that the company could pull it off; they did and *Black Comedy*, tailor-made for that particular group of players, became one of the greatest successes of the repertory. That had been in 1966, the end of which year saw first a faltering, with an unsatisfactory production of Ostrovsky's masterpiece *The Storm*, and a curious version by John Osborne of a Lope de Vega play, *A Bond Honoured*. 1967 marked some sort of a watershed for the company. The year opened strongly with Stoppard's *Rosencrantz and Guildenstern Are Dead*, Tynan's discovery from the Edinburgh Festival, *Three Sisters* directed by Olivier, and the all-male *As You Like It*, a somewhat modish presentation directed by Clifford Williams. The idea behind the production had originated in a far more sexually provocative form with John Dexter, who resigned when Olivier tried to dilute his original, polymorphously perverse, vision, all sexual ambiguity and alternative philosophy. Dexter's departure removed the last strong Royal Court presence from the company, Gaskill having returned to take the helm in Sloane Square on the death of George Devine. *As You Like It* was a box-office success, but then there was a sequence of miscalculations during which the company not merely lost its way, but seemed to some extent to have lost its identity: two uninspired productions by a now ailing Tyrone Guthrie, one of which at last brought John Gielgud to the National. But Orgon in *Tartuffe* was never going to be his part, any more than Oedipus in Seneca's play,

Main picture: Robert Stephens and Laurence Olivier in *The Recruiting Officer*, 1964 (Photo: Lewis Morley)

Top right: Jeremy Brett and Ronald Pickup in *As You Like It*, 1967 (Photo: Zoë Dominic)

Below right: Derek Jacobi and Albert Finney in *Black Comedy*, 1966 (Photo: Lewis Morley)

which followed.

The latter was given a startling production by Peter Brook, visionary and harrowing, but, despite the presence in it of Colin Blakely, one of the great stalwarts of Olivier's core group of actors, it had the air of work grafted on to the repertory rather than having evolved out of the company; Irene Worth, an old associate of Brook's, was a consummate Jocasta, but this was her single performance with the National Theatre at the Old Vic. An ugly little row between Olivier and Brook over the latter's desire to end the evening with a performance by jazz band of the National Anthem (still, in 1968, played every night after the show) contrapuntally intertwined with 'Yes, We Have No Bananas', somehow assumed a significance out of all proportion to its importance. Olivier's patriotic instincts, to say nothing of his sense of *lèse-majesté*, were profoundly offended by Brook's suggestion, and he resolved the matter somewhat huffily by suspending all playing of 'God Save The Queen' for the future. There was a sense of Olivier having been, not merely out-manoeuvred, but revealed as old-fashioned and old-fogey. The psychological effect on Olivier was profound; and, like a tribal community, the company was affected by whatever affected the leader. "Like a defeated boxer, I knew I should remember it as the punch that started my undoing," he wrote in his *Confessions*. The confrontation also highlighted a problem inherent in a company without a formal aesthetic, one largely built, in terms both of repertoire and personnel, on the taste of a group of individuals: to what extent was the company still itself, even when executing the will of an outside director, someone with a highly evolved aesthetic of his own? Had Olivier himself appeared in the production, this dilemma might have been resolved, or at least side-stepped; but now the questions of what the company was, what it stood for, and how it would develop, posed itself in several different ways, specially vital questions in the light of the new building's imminence.

To relieve some of the administrative pressure and to prepare the company for its move to new premises, Frank Dunlop had been appointed Administrative Director in 1967, on the strength of a varied track record which included running several companies: he was a co-founding director of the Nottingham Playhouse and had worked closely with Bernard Miles at the Mermaid; perhaps most significantly, he had created Pop Theatre, with whom he had staged a number of lively, jazzy Shakespearean revivals. His first production for the company was *Edward II* – the Brecht adaptation, rather than the Marlowe original that might have been expected from the National Theatre of Great Britain – and a good solid Berliner Ensemble-style job he made of it, with rough textures, the statutory revolve and expressionist make-ups, but it seemed a curious exercise in theatrical historicism. Something of the chemical excitement that had characterised the work of the company's first years was absent. Another questionable experiment was a Triple Bill directed by actors, two from within the company, Robert Lang and Robert Stephens, and one who had had no previous or subsequent connection with it, Victor Spinetti – an experiment which foundered on the choice of materials (minor pieces by Fielding and the Victorian John Madison Morton, plus an adaptation of John Lennon's *jeu d'esprit*, *In His Own Write*), and on a certain lack of confidence on the part of the actor-directors. This did not seem to be a way forward, nor did it succeed in its intention of keeping the actors happy, an objective which was pursued with increasing, and increasingly unsuccessful, urgency.

The key problem, as Tynan expressed it in a memo to Olivier, was that it now seemed that "the purpose of keeping the company together is merely to keep the company

John Stride and
Edward Petherbridge
in *Rosencrantz and
Guildenstern Are Dead*, 1967
(Photo: Anthony Crickmay)

together." The critical question of the company and its relation to the work had been the subject of a memo dated as early as October 1964 from Tynan to Olivier, headed Reflections on Year One: "one thing the season has proved is the immense difficulty of creating a permanent ensemble when the terms of reference are so wide.... I think," he said, in a spectacular withdrawal from the very ideal of the ensemble, "it is possible that the 'guest performer' principle may have to be a permanent part of our policy." The repertoire, too, seemed increasingly arbitrary: *The Advertisement*, an international prize-winning play of no discernible merit whatever; *Home and Beauty*, a piece of boulevard fluff by Somerset Maugham; a strangely subdued *Love's Labour's Lost* directed by Olivier in a chocolate-box, Christmas-card sort of décor in a misplaced reminiscence of Brook's Watteau-esque Stratford production of nearly twenty years before. As an actor, Olivier himself had, in 1967, created a major new rôle in *The Dance of Death*, one of his most unsparing and greatest performances, ruthlessly self-revealed, and it remained in the repertoire for some years. He also continued to appear, in the best actor-managerial traditions, as a replacement for other actors in unscheduled and uncredited appearances – identified in the programme, in that same actor-managerial tradition, as 'Walter Plinge'. He continued to do this despite the fact that he was in poor physical health, that his memory was increasingly unreliable and that he had for some years now – since he had taken over the rôle of Solness from Michael Redgrave – been afflicted by devastating stage-fright. Through much of his two-year stint in *Othello*, his fellow actors were asked never to look him in the eyes, and never to leave him alone on stage. Despite all this, he insisted on leading from the front; he knew no other way, but the effect on the company was not always altogether inspiring.

Tynan, too, was in poor health: his suicidal commitment to nicotine had resulted in emphysema, and he was to take leave of absence in 1969. The Board – which to all intents and purposes meant Oliver Chandos, who had always resented Tynan's impertinent independence – seized the moment to humble him: when he returned from his leave he would no longer be known as Literary Manager, but as Literary Consultant, a title which he would share with his *locum tenens*, Derek Granger. The practical effect of this was insignificant; though he and his department had worked exceptionally hard sifting, screening, and sometimes censoring scripts, Tynan had functioned neither as manager nor as consultant, operating rather as a sort of general conscience, arbiter of taste and occasional fixer. His membership of the international jet-set initiated several projects, including some that remained tantalisingly unrealised (*The Bacchae* directed by Jerome Robbins; *Long Day's Journey Into Night* directed by Mike Nichols) – and he continued after his return to offer his advice on every topic under the sun, much of it trenchant and germane, some of it less so, especially when it came from the radical-chic perspective that was part of his complex persona. However, the change of title was not without its resonance in psychological terms, both for Tynan and for Olivier, his only real supporter within the organisation. Tynan had been marked down by Chandos as Public Enemy Number One since his attempt to introduce *Soldiers*, Rolf Hochhuth's saga of the ethics of war, into the repertory. Olivier himself was, to say the least, ambivalent about presenting a play which suggested that Churchill had authorised the death of the Polish air force hero, General Sikorski, but Tynan had won him over by the argument, irresistible to him, that the RSC was stealing a march over the National by staging plays – like Peter Brook's production of *Tell Me Lies* or Clifford Williams's of Hochhuth's *The Representative* – which boldly addressed contemporary issues. "What the National

Theatre does," Tynan wrote in a memo, "has become a matter of public acceptance rather than public excitement...we are doing nothing to remind them that the theatre is an independent force at the heart of a country's life – a sleeping tiger that can and should be roused whenever the national or international conscience needs nudging." And it was true that the National Theatre, despite a number of successes with new plays, had not taken any steps towards what Olivier had dreamed of in 1946 – "special playwrights' schools attached to theatres in much the same way that some theatres possess dramatic academies for their acting students" – and had steered clear of the more contentious political writing which by now was making most of the running in the avant-garde of British Theatre.

As he so often did – and so much enjoyed doing – Tynan had walked straight into the lion's den with his promotion of *Soldiers*. Firstly, Churchill's former colleague Chandos was enraged at the very notion of his old boss being criticised; that the criticism should come from the stage of the National Theatre, the National Theatre that he had fought for so many years to establish, was doubly intolerable. Olivier would not have been the head of the National Theatre had he, Chandos, not made it happen, and now this. It was an outrage. Two great issues raised their heads: what was the National Theatre for? And who was in charge? Olivier was, frankly, out of his depth. It was as if Buckingham had rounded on Richard III after the coronation. Tynan fired off witty memo after witty memo, and contrived almost daily leaks to the press, but Olivier was unwilling to defy Chandos (until it was too late, when he finally had him removed in 1972). In 1966, he surrendered on the matter of *Soldiers*, and the aftermath of that left a number of uneasy relations – with the Board, with Tynan and with himself. It had been the second such defeat: the Lord Chamberlain, still, in 1965, censor of plays for a few more ludicrous years, had made it impossible for the National Theatre to stage Wedekind's *Spring Awakening*, but Olivier and Tynan and their associates had not made an issue of that. With *Soldiers* they had, and they had lost. For the time being, Chandos had succeeded in his determination to make the National Theatre the official face of British theatrical culture. Each régime at the National Theatre was to have its scandal; *Soldiers* was Olivier's. His successors were able to learn by the outcome of this one, and to benefit from it, but it was in no uncertain terms a débâcle at the time, and left the questions of the purpose of the National Theatre and its autonomy uneasily unanswered.

It says much for Olivier's fortitude and his sheer staying power that despite poor physical health, and an increasingly vulnerable psychological condition – pushed this way by Tynan and that way by Chandos, neither of whom actually had to run the theatre, not to mention direct plays or act in them – that he was so prodigiously and industriously effective on so many fronts. A great deal of his time was taken up with a matter that had been on the top of his agenda from the very first: that of the new building. The moment his directorship had been announced, a committee of immensely distinguished theatre practitioners – directors, mostly: Hall, Brook, St Denis, Dexter, Gaskill and Devine among others, but including a number of designers and two actors, Olivier and Robert Stephens – set out to find the most suitable architect for the job, and then to brief him on the sort of building that would satisfy all the many criteria demanded by this extraordinary enterprise, both practical and symbolic. Olivier threw himself into the process with the passion of a man who believes he is constructing his own monument. This, surely, would establish beyond any question his central rôle in the British Theatre. As Peter Hall confided to his diary when he contemplated the nearly finished building,

Olivier with Denys Lasdun, architect of the new National Theatre, 1967 (Photo: Keystone)

Oliver Lyttelton, Viscount Chandos, first Chairman of the National Theatre Board (Photo: Crispian Woodgate)

A plan of the Olivier Theatre with (*left*) Lasdun's original sketch of "a room with a stage in the corner"

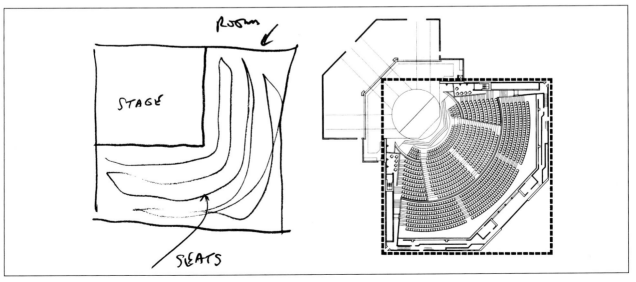

"Larry, Czar of the stage, was determined to design a theatre grander and more beautifully equipped than any in history..." The echo of Ozymandias in this phrase seems entirely appropriate. It was the quest of the consultants, spurred on by Olivier, to create a theatre that would out-theatre all theatres; that would be at once ultra-modern and also firmly plugged into the ritual roots of theatre; that would be adaptable to any form of play, from any period of history; and that would be a thing of beauty in itself, a beacon, a temple and a fun palace all rolled into one, a sort of triumphal arch of the theatre, all things to all men and women of the theatre.

It is all the more extraordinary that the architect unanimously and enthusiastically chosen to execute this impossible brief should have been Denys Lasdun. Not on grounds of architectural distinction – he was among the most admired practitioners of his generation – but because he had never designed a theatre in his life. For some almost inexplicable reason, this was regarded as an admirable quality by the distinguished theatre men and women who chose him. Perhaps they thought that they would usher in a revolutionary era of miraculously clear acoustics and thrillingly direct relationship between stage and audience, exceeding everything the Georgian, Victorian and Edwardian theatre architects had achieved; or perhaps he had cleverly played to their vanity. "The committee was particularly impressed," wrote Lord Cottesloe, the chairman of the Arts Council, and instrumental in facilitating the co-ordination of government and GLC funding of the building, "when he said that he knew nothing about designing theatres and would have to sit down and learn what was needed from our committee." It was determined that three auditoriums were required: a small experimental theatre, a somewhat larger proscenium arch theatre, and an epic main house, the central and most radical of the spaces. Enormous energy went into determining exactly what might be the appropriate shape for this large auditorium; eventually, in a moment of revelation, Lasdun said: "what you want is a room with a stage in the corner" and that is what, to universal delight ("all the members of the committee are immensely happy with this concept," reported Olivier) he designed, and that is what, in the fullness of time, he built.

So much for planning; the practical realities of the building were in the future. Lasdun's designs were finally delivered in 1966. But the unending meetings, the relocation of the planned site, the labour shortages, the rising cost of energy and the subsequent lobbying of government for funds to erect a building that had been guaranteed by Parliamentary Bill nearly twenty years previously, continued drainingly, year in and year out. Olivier saw his dream of leading the company into its theatrical Valhalla fade further and further. The work of the company continued at the Old Vic rather uncertainly with a dutiful production of an unmercifully full-length version of *Back to Methuselah*, and a couple of unhappy productions: *The Idiot* and *Cyrano de Bergerac*. But the arrival of Peter Nichols's mordant satire *The National Health*, in a dazzling production by Michael Blakemore, was an encouraging symptom of the National's own health, ushering in a period of considerable brilliance with the return of Maggie Smith, equally definitive in Ibsen and Farquhar, and a fine *Mrs Warren's Profession*. The impression was of a series of brilliant achievements by great soloists who had come to work with the company – Coral Browne in the Shaw, for example, and even Maggie Smith in *Hedda Gabler* and *The Beaux' Stratagem*, who seemed to be returning as a visitor, rather than as part of the company. It was left to Olivier, heroically, given his by now almost incapacitating stage fright, to galvanise the company into a sense of purpose and identity, assuming a rôle he had never cared for, Shylock, in a witty and original

Maggie Smith as Hedda Gabler, 1970 (Photo: Zoë Dominic)

26

production by Jonathan Miller – a director very much after Olivier's heart, like him a committed "glamouriser of thought". With a cast of stalwarts old and new – Joan Plowright, Anthony Nicholls, Derek Jacobi, Anna Carteret, Jane Lapotaire among the former, Jeremy Brett and Jim Dale among the latter, and, right at the centre, an unmistakably great performance – the production seemed to belong to the great line of work at the National Theatre: physically and sensuously exciting, intellectually provocative, at once seductive and challenging, and directly communicative with the audience. Olivier was above all a great communicator; there was not a touch of mystery about him. One of his many definitions of acting was as "the art of persuasion". As Tynan had said in a very early memo to Olivier: "we want a theatre of intelligent audiences...I thought we had outgrown the idea of theatre as a mystic rite born of secret communion between author, director, actors and an empty auditorium." This concept of the critical audience was common to Tynan and Olivier; the latter had expressed his desire to "interest the public in the idea of acting...so that eventually, perhaps, the art of the actor may finally be regarded as an important part of the life of the people." An interesting symptom of this attitude was the publication by the National Theatre (in 1972) of a survey of its productions so far by the then theatre critic of the *Observer*, Robert Cushman, which, while endorsing and celebrating the work of the company, was frankly critical of certain productions and performances – an unusual procedure in an official publication, but a refreshing one, which suggested a degree of openness and a conviction that the audience might follow the fortunes of its favourite theatre with the sort of informed and critical enthusiasm characteristic of cricket supporters or racing followers.

The question of the strength of the ensemble was a necessary obsession of Olivier and Tynan, and, perforce, of their successors. The great ensembles by whom they had been inspired maintained large companies on permanent contracts, with occasional leaves of absence; very often the actors were recruited from drama schools attached to the companies, and they would remain with them till they retired, so they would indeed spend their entire artistic lives with the same organisation. This was not a pattern which had ever been part of the British tradition, and there was little chance of its being adopted; but how to ensure that there was at the very least a continuity, and strength from top to bottom of a cast, while avoiding what might be called the curse of the old lag? In Britain the blandishments of television and, increasingly, of Hollywood were a constant threat – a threat unknown for the most part in European countries, where the indigenous film industry does not require transplantation to the other side of the globe; a career in both film and theatre in Germany, Italy or France was perfectly possible, as it had been in Britain in the thirties. The salaries offered by the British National Theatre were well below what could be earned in the West End; for an actor in mid-career, at the peak of his earning potential, and with all the usual commitments, the financial rewards of membership of the company were risible, amounting to a form of individual subsidy on the part of the actor. For the first five years of the company's existence, the glory and the glamour associated with Olivier and his great enterprise were compensation enough; but then harder-nosed considerations began to apply, and it became difficult to apply the principles of nurture and gradual advancement that had been so effectively practised in those first years. There was now a much more *ad hoc* feel to the company. Gaskill and Dexter had never been effectively replaced as company trainers, hands-on mechanics of the acting process, who saw themselves as much teachers as directors. This lack of

Pavement to scaffolding: Laurence Olivier, Joan Plowright, Anthony Nicholls, Jane Lapotaire, Jim Dale, Jeremy Brett, photographed outside the Cambridge Theatre before the Company's season there, 1970 (Photo: Keystone)

continuity from the associate directors contributed to the lack of cohesion, despite occasional brilliant performances at all levels of the company. An ensemble does not require a common political or philosophical outlook, but it does require a commitment to a specific approach to work; the National Theatre at the Old Vic was, from the seventies, lacking in that commitment – or indeed, in that approach.

Olivier was frequently criticised for refusing to work with his great contemporaries, for fear, it was said, of the competition, and though his *Uncle Vanya* and *Hamlet* had been starry enough, there was, no doubt, a certain reluctance to share with his contemporaries the glory in what he thought of as very much *his* theatre. His declared intention of developing a new breed of actors – in his mould, physically, vocally and in interpretative daring – had the happy advantage for him that he was in a league of his own. He called off – quite legitimately, on grounds of ill health – the eagerly-awaited acting duel between himself and John Gielgud in *The Pretenders,* and in fact, with the exceptions of Constance Cummings in *Long Day's Journey Into Night* and Redgrave in *Vanya,* never acted with his peers during his time at the National Theatre. When great actors came to the National, it was generally for brief stays in a rôle or two like Gielgud, and, later, Paul Scofield. (Scofield joined the company as Associate Director, but quietly resigned after only his second part, in the slight Pirandello play *The Rules of the Game,* despite having, in his first role with the company, given one of the greatest performances of his – or anyone's – career in *The Captain of Köpenick*). But Olivier was passionately and practically devoted to developing younger actors, and as long as he was able to attract the strongest young talent, his policy carried within it the potential of developing a powerful and independent group.

To show that a sense of ensemble was still within grasp, Dexter returned to stage *A Woman Killed With Kindness,* with Anthony Hopkins and Joan Plowright in the leading roles, and it was as if the clock had been turned back to those early, heroic days. But this coincided with the company's most confused period so far, when, ever-mindful of the need to expand in readiness for the occupation of the new building – despite the unending delays – two West End seasons had been mounted, with an ambitious and erratic repertory. The season at the Cambridge was up to a point successful, but the one at the New – scene of so many past glories – was a disaster, only saved, in the final reel, by Olivier. Fully recovered, after just four months of a predicted year-long recuperation, from the thrombosis which had forced him to cede the role of Shylock to Robert Lang, he gave a supremely commanding, physically daring performance as James Tyrone in *Long Day's Journey Into Night,* with Constance Cummings, Denis Quilley and Ronald Pickup matching him, blow for blow.

It was the last time he would be able to pull that particular rabbit out of the hat; his last great rôle, his last monumental effort of will. His health was now imperilling his capacity to run the theatre with full vigour; and the new chairman of the Board, Max Rayne (Chandos having been finally and effortlessly despatched by Arnold Goodman, now Chairman of the Arts Council), proved quite as determined as his predecessor, if in a less flamboyantly confrontational fashion. He immediately started taking quiet soundings for a potential successor to Olivier. Olivier, though still longing to lead the company into the great shrine on the South Bank, was by now profoundly battle-weary, exhausted by the unending delays to the new building. He received a fresh humiliation from the Board in the form of the cancellation of his much-cherished dream, the long-mooted production of *Guys and Dolls* (an inspiration of Tynan's), to be directed by

Top: Malcolm Reid, Paul Scofield and John Moffatt in *The Captain of Köpenick,* 1971 (Photo: Reg Wilson)

Below: Laurence Olivier, Constance Cummings, Denis Quilley and Ronald Pickup in *Long Day's Journey Into Night,* 1971 (Photo: Zoë Dominic)

Garson Kanin, with Olivier himself as Nathan Detroit. The company and Olivier had been joyfully and rigorously preparing themselves, taking singing and dancing lessons for what looked like a sure-fire triumph, but they were overruled on financial grounds, and glumness descended over the whole organisation for a while.

Then – in the way of things – the Company experienced a brilliant upswing in its fortunes; a succession of dazzling productions by its team of resident directors, Jonathan Miller, John Dexter and Michael Blakemore, an ill-assorted group who nonetheless worked happily and fruitfully in tandem with each other and Olivier. Indeed, in 1972-73 they seemed a world-beating team: Dexter's *Misanthrope* and *Equus*, Blakemore's *Front Page* and Miller's *School for Scandal* made a formidable string of successes, very much in the vein of the triumphs of the Olivier régime, glamorous, sexy, stylish and provocative. Add Stoppard's *Jumpers*, and de Filippo's *Saturday, Sunday, Monday* directed, respectively, by Peter Wood and Franco Zeffirelli, with a company which included Denis Quilley, Diana Rigg, Alec McCowen, Joan Plowright, Frank Finlay, with a great deal of strength in smaller parts (including Olivier himself as the grandfather in the de Filippo) and one might have been forgiven for thinking that the National Theatre at the Old Vic was enjoying a golden period. Despite the fluctuations in the strength of the company, it was still possible to engender work of the liveliest quality. The problem was not continuity – because the 72-73 season was a judicious mix of old hands and new – but growth and stability.

For Olivier himself, the golden glow of that season was shadowed by his final acknowledgement that he had to give up not only running the company but also acting on stage; he was only 65, but burnt out by the incessant, superhuman demands he had made on his mind and body. In 1973, he performed the topping-out ceremony for the new building (though the opening date was yet again shifted, this time to April 1975) knowing that he would never act in it, or direct in it, or even have an office in it. When he discovered the name of his successor, however, resignation and exhaustion gave way to rage. The manner of his succession seems to have been somewhat conspiratorial – a Shakespearean affair, in the manner of *Julius Caesar*, consisting of whispered meetings in corridors, nods and winks, alliances and vows of secrecy – but Olivier's rage against the Board, or Peter Hall, who had been chosen, secretly but unanimously, to follow him, was misdirected. Time and circumstance had defeated him – these and his own body. It was a pitiful spectacle, nonetheless, Lear-like, in fact, a king grown old before his time, a plaything of the unjust gods. He withdrew from the Old Vic as soon as he possibly could, after a brief interregnum while he and Peter Hall ran the theatre together, and was not seen again till the royal opening of the new building.

His achievements during the ten years in which he ran the theatre were exceptional, both personally – his performances and his productions – and in his quality of leadership. He chose, especially in the early years, remarkable collaborators, actors, designers, administrators, technicians; the talented individuals whom he identified and encouraged have all gone on to great triumphs in their respective fields. He put the National Theatre on the map in no uncertain terms, creating an organisation that was at once a centre of theatrical excellence, a symbol of national pride, and a focus for the aspirations of the profession, and he gave it a character quite different from that of either the Royal Shakespeare Company or any commercial management. He brought a quality to the theatre, both in its artistic output and its style, that can best be described as sexiness, making the stage both magnetic and incandescent; what the work lacked in *gravitas* or

Clockwise from top left:
Denis Quilley and Alan MacNaughtan in *The Front Page*, 1972 (Photo: Sophie Baker)

Peter Firth and Nicholas Clay in *Equus*, 1973 (Photo: John Haynes)

Joan Plowright and Laurence Olivier in *Saturday Sunday Monday*, 1973 (Photo: Zoë Dominic)

Diana Rigg and Michael Hordern in *Jumpers* (Photo: Zoë Dominic)

intellectual toughness, it usually made up for in flair and immediacy – in communication. Olivier's performances celebrated the word made flesh, and so did his theatre.

It seems clear now, however, that what he and his collaborators did at the Old Vic was the glorious end of an era rather than the beginning of one. It was the gallant last flourish of the actor-manager, at the head of his family of troupers; it was the end of the one-man band. More romantically, it was the end of the theatre as a raffish, Bohemian activity; the end of heroic efforts waged against impossible odds. From now on, it was no more Once More Unto the Breach, Dear Friends, or Cry God for Larry, England and St George; now it was the theatre as a serious, responsible enterprise, run on sound business principles, properly endowed, systematically engaging with the drama of the past and the present, and taking its place among the great institutions of this great nation. The abiding image of Olivier and the National Theatre at the Old Vic is one of gallantry, of an exceptional man, a king among men, motivated by a number of old-fashioned imperatives, including vanity, patriotism, love of the theatre and an unashamed craving for good notices from posterity, who weighed in to a task which was virtually impossible for one man to accomplish, who was caught in every kind of crossfire, from within and without, and who to a large extent nonetheless succeeded, at the cost of his own health and career. Olivier could be several kinds of a demon, as he himself admitted, but what he did at the National Theatre was as close to complete self-sacrifice as he ever came, and the blazing success of his tenure was like a glorious and sustained fanfare for the more measured and solid achievements that were to follow. And bitterly though he regretted it, it seems wholly appropriate that he should not have led his company into the great grey mausoleum that he had himself brought into being.

Peter Hall: Empire Builder

The man who succeeded him in 1973 was of an utterly different cast. Peter Hall was much younger, at 45 years old no longer a *wunderkind*, but fresh and full of fight, already a central figure in the British theatre. His creation of the Royal Shakespeare Company thirteen years before had been a milestone in the history of Britain's relationship to its greatest writer, affording a sustained exploration of the canon at a level never before attempted. It far outstripped, in production values and unified company work, any previous attempts, even at the Old Vic or the Shakespeare Memorial Theatre, on whose distinguished annual seasons his new company had been built. It was Hall who saw the potential for extending those seasons into a continuous programme with a permanent group, to create an organisation on a par with the great continental theatres, the Comédie Française, or the Berliner Ensemble. He was insistent, too, that there should be a London showcase for the productions, and that new plays and classics by authors other than the company's eponymous dramatist should be staged, to ensure that the Shakespearean repertory was constantly refreshed by contact with other theatrical intelligences. He saw all this very clearly, and he made it happen by brilliantly skilful manoeuvring. Unlike Olivier, Hall was a natural politician; he was, too, unlike the older man, naturally comfortable within a large organisation.

If Olivier was a king, Hall was an emperor, and it had been his instinct from the very earliest days, to build empires. His first – small in scale, but an empire nonetheless – was at the Arts Theatre, where for some years he ran his dynamic and innovative seasons, directing, amongst other bold things, the English-language premiere of *Waiting for Godot*. While still at the Arts, he started working at Stratford-upon-Avon, at a time when expansion was in the air. It was his sense of organisation, his gift for planning, and his

Peter Hall in rehearsal, 1973
(Photo: Anthony Crickmay)

practical determination and energy, not to mention his sheer and perfectly honourable ambition (at the Arts, he had turned to his assistant Tomàs macAnna and said "Tom, you and I are both the sons of station masters. In ten years time, I shall be running the British theatre. What will you be doing?") which made him a clear candidate to take over the Stratford company from the distinguished actor-manager Anthony Quayle, who had laid the foundations for that expansion. More important even than any of those sterling qualities was his powerful theatrical instinct, always rooted in his sense of the text. For him the text was *fons et origo* of the whole dramatic experience; the theatrical effect was secondary to the scrupulous engagement with the meaning of the words, and their music. Deeply musical himself, he always looked for what was inherent in the material, rather than seeing what opportunities it afforded to impose something on it. Lacking either the flamboyant choreographic brilliance of a Guthrie, the experimental audacity of a Brook or the physical daring of an Olivier, he constantly sought the hard-won insights that could only arise from an intense enquiry into the text and a mature appreciation of its form.

In the early years of the Royal Shakespeare Company, he brought to this an urgent political attitude, and pulled first *Hamlet* then *The Wars of the Roses*, into the political arena, often, with his colleague and mentor John Barton at his side, rewriting the texts for greater clarity and structural coherence. Barton, an extraordinary combination of profound scholar and theatrical wizard, was often, despite his monkish appearance and donnish manner, and his reputation as the Guardian of the Text, more theatrically daring than all his colleagues put together, Hall included, and a great deal of Hall's work during these years bore the mark of his influence, as if Barton had given him a sort of scholarly imprimatur, licence not to be strictly correct. Barton was a key figure for him, occupying a not dissimilar position in relation to him that Tynan had to Olivier, but for utterly different reasons. Hall had no lack of intellectual confidence; indeed, all his confidence came from his intellect. What he needed was courage to experiment, to let his subconscious have its say. He surrounded himself with directors – without exception university graduates like himself – engaged with the great intellectual issues posed by the plays, but each of whom had a style and approach of his own: John Barton, Peter Wood, Peter Brook. Hall's head of design, John Bury, was from a non-academic tradition – that of Joan Littlewood at the Theatre Workshop – but in his work with Hall he evolved a language of design which was linear, epic and rough in surface. It was as far from campness, whether high, medium or low, as could conceivably be arranged. The actors that Hall chose were striking above all for their sense of integrity. If one person could be said to exemplify everything that Peter Hall wanted from an actor, that person was Peggy Ashcroft, whose luminous spirit, fearlessness, lack of star temperament, and absolute commitment to the ensemble, were at the core of all Hall's work with the Company. Showiness or bravura were not requirements, nor indeed advantages. Physical excitement was present, but not of the athletic variety so much promoted and encouraged by Olivier. A degree of realism prevailed, to a frightening extent, in the work of Peter Brook, which represented, in the *Marat/Sade*, for example, a depiction of insanity of a clinical accuracy never before seen on the English stage. This was a new kind of startling austerity, a brutality, deriving to some extent from his embrace of Artaud. A sacerdotal element, too, now entered into Brook's work, though not into that of Hall.

There was a palpable seriousness of tone about the Royal Shakespeare Company which justifies Tynan's delineation of Hall's organisation as being essentially Roundhead. It did not preclude comedy – far from it: Scofield's *Government Inspector*, for example was

Top: Wendy Hiller in *John Gabriel Borkman*, 1975 (Photo: Zoë Dominic)

Below: Laurence Olivier, John Gielgud, Ralph Richardson, Peggy Ashcroft and Peter Hall celebrating Gielgud's 70th birthday in April 1974 (Photo: Nobby Clark)

riotously funny – but it was not frivolous. Much of this derives from Hall; part of its provenance is in a profoundly unmetropolitan quality to the man, a sense of his roots in the country. His work was always striving towards some sort of reconstitution of the ideals of community. The body politic was his invariable subject, whether in Shakespeare or in Pinter (with his sense of ravaged communities, small or large), and in fact, in the Royal Shakespeare Company he had created a sort of community, an elaborate organisation of which he was the Elder; a very young elder, to be sure, but invested with a powerful authority bound up with what he had created. He was an infinitely subtler operator than Olivier, whose charm and inspirational qualities stopped short of real strategy. Legends already abounded about Hall's Machiavellian skills, but, within certain undisputed parameters – there was never any question of who was in charge – he was capable of flexibility, sometimes displaying an unexpected degree of vulnerability; moreover, his skills were wholly at the disposal of Shakespeare and the company, not of himself. If the succession to the leadership of the National Theatre suggested Shakespearean models, and if Olivier was, at any one time, either Henry V, Richard III, or King Lear, then Hall was the Duke in *Measure for Measure* – before retirement from the scene, of course.

He was as clearly as Olivier had been before him the right, and in fact pretty nearly the inevitable, choice for the job. Olivier had cheekily invited him to be his No. 2 when he founded the company; even then (when he was in his early 30s) the idea of Peter Hall as No. 2 to anybody was hilarious, and he had politely declined ("I want to be my own No. 1.") He had left the RSC after nine years, appointing his own successor, Trevor Nunn – as young then as he himself had been when he created the company. He had then gone on to the Royal Opera House, a job from which he had resigned when it became clear that he would be unable to reform it: another empire, but a ramshackle, Byzantine empire of empires within an empire. His operatic work was increasingly important to him as a director, and this began to show in his work in the dramatic theatre, but the Royal Opera House was not to be his chosen stamping ground. For the moment, he was an unemployed Emperor, and there was a vacancy for one at the National Theatre. Olivier had desperately wanted to be succeeded by an actor, but not only was the job of running the new National incompatible with the physical and emotional demands of playing great rôles: there was now no-one who wanted to do so. Olivier's generation were all by now too old, and the next generation – Finney, Stephens, Plowright (Olivier's especial favourite to succeed him) – were simply not interested. Perhaps there was an element of fear, too; Olivier proved, just as he had intended, in every sense an impossible act to follow. In addition, though, heading a large, subsidised theatre company was simply no longer something an actor wanted to do (except, for a brief moment before film-making seduced him away, in the case of Kenneth Branagh, who might indeed be the only conceivable actor-managing candidate for the future). There was a tacit understanding that theatres, certainly on this scale, were now institutions, and actors had no business running them, just as Guthrie had insisted thirty years before. Not that many directors, for that matter, were interested in the physically exhausting work required. It demanded a combination of stamina, guile, appetite for the fray, ambition and sheer public-spiritedness possessed by few; the candidate had to be of a certain stature as an artist, carry great personal authority, and be willing to devote himself to the organisation and its needs at least 24 hours a day. Peter Hall was such a man, and there were few others. Having failed to interest an actor in the job, Olivier nominated Michael Blakemore, a

The new building under construction, 1971 (Photo: C W P Holmes)

director (and sometime actor) of exceptional skill, who had run the Citizens' Theatre in Glasgow with great flair. Whether he would have been able or willing to take on the vast challenge of running what the National Theatre was destined to become, is an interesting question, but the Board felt him to be underqualified; in the event he joined Jonathan Miller and John Dexter as co-directors of the company under the new regime of which Hall now assumed control. Olivier did his best to accept the *fait accompli* with good grace, but he always bitterly resented the manner in which the succession had been determined, and to a certain extent resented his successor, whom he had never for a moment suspected of having designs on *his* National Theatre. Both he and Tynan feared that Hall would simply turn the theatre they had strived so hard to endow with a particular character into the RSC Mark II; Tynan argued that it was not a change of course that was needed, but an evolution: "as Mr Hall evolved out of the previous Stratford régime, as Trevor Nunn evolved out of his." Interestingly Hall made only one absolutely clear condition in terms of personnel before assuming the directorship: that he would not work with Tynan. It was clear, to themselves as much as to others, that the two men would have nothing in common, and Tynan took his dismissal philosophically, merely noting the inevitable loss of identity which the National Theatre would endure in being taken over by the founder of its principal rival. In fact, this particular anxiety proved misplaced, partly because Hall, though he brought many of his former colleagues with him, had evolved some way from his earlier self, both aesthetically and personally, but mostly because, in the event, it was the building and its demands which set the agenda.

The building immediately loomed very large indeed – not physically, yet, because its opening was postponed yet again – but because of the unprecedented scale of its demand for productions. Work continued at the Vic for another three years, but at the back of everyone's mind was not the theatre in which the shows were actually taking place, but the ones for which they were destined. In the event, as the opening date of the new building receded further and further, many of them never made it and lived and died at the Old Vic, which was possibly just as well, since the last years there were of distinctly mixed quality. It was a self-evidently transitional period. Hall made a bold opening statement of his own with *The Tempest*, featuring John Gielgud as Prospero, a piece of casting which was something of a statement in its own right: in contrast to Olivier's company, this would be a theatre of heavyweight classical talents. Gielgud, Richardson, Peggy Ashcroft and Wendy Hiller all appeared at the Vic within the next couple of years, exactly the sort of casting that many people had been urging on Olivier from the very start. The production of *The Tempest* was not entirely successful, but it gave notice of a change in Hall's approach. He had now come to believe that form was the royal road to content; concluding that the play was essentially a masque, he staged it accordingly, with much machinery and many apparitions, but without much urgency. There was something soporific about the experience, which infected even that most mercurial of actors, Gielgud: clearly made up to resemble John Dee, he was rather forced into embodying The Magus rather than playing the character. The production had the aura of High Art about it, something of which Olivier could never have been accused. Olivier's old team, alas, scarcely made much better showing: Miller's *Marriage of Figaro*, crippled by the withdrawal of Ian Holm, was dull, his *Freeway*, a new Peter Nichols play, was rambling, though his pared-down, echt-Viennese, Mobile production of *Measure for Measure* was original and powerful. Blakemore's *Grand Manoeuvres*, about the Dreyfus case, was thin and long, and Olivier's own production of *Eden End*, his last work for the

John Gielgud and Michael Feast in *The Tempest*, 1974 (Photo: Zoë Dominic)

company as a director, was routine. He himself went out with some glory as an actor, however, playing the part of the Glaswegian revolutionary John Tagg in Trevor Griffiths's *The Party*, a figure based on Gerry Healey, the leader of the Workers' Revolutionary Party. Olivier handled Tagg's immensely long analytical speech at the heart of the play with his usual bravura, betraying no evidence of the monstrous effort it had cost him to learn the part. It was to be his last performance on any stage. (There is a charming anecdote about Olivier in conjunction with this last of all his stage performances: Griffiths was a little surprised to receive a call from the notoriously politically conservative Olivier, saying how thrilled and challenged he was to be playing the fiercely radical Tagg. "You see," he told the playwright, "I've never played a Scotsman before.") The production itself (Dexter's) was somewhat uncertain in tone, seeming to focus excessively on sexual politics at the expense of the dialectic in a rather overblown staging which drew away from the play's uncompromising argument.

Hall's incoming team offered *Spring Awakening* at last, but in a curiously clinical production by Bill Bryden (whose work both as a playwright and director naturally appealed to Hall's taste for theatre which celebrated the life of the community), and John Hopkins's *Next of Kin* – directed by Hall's friend and close colleague Harold Pinter – restrained and powerful, but ultimately treading familiar ground in a familiar manner. In the following year, however, something like a house style began to emerge, with a stupendous production by Hall of *John Gabriel Borkman*, stupendously cast, with Ralph Richardson at his towering greatest, and Wendy Hiller and Peggy Ashcroft not far behind, and a *Heartbreak House*, directed by John Schlesinger, headed by Colin Blakely and Eileen Atkins. Both productions had a kind of luxurious, highly-polished quality that was not unlike the very best West End work of a certain period (the forties and fifties), a tone and standard which continued into the new building, creating something of a feeling of H M Tennent on the South Bank. Admirable in itself, it was somewhat lacking in individual tone, something the productions of the Olivier years – good or bad – had never failed to possess. Of that tone, here were two last examples, both unsatisfactory: Dexter's *Phaedra Britannica* adapted by Tony Harrison (the *Misanthrope* team stumbling with Racine) and Blakemore's camped-up production of W.S. Gilbert's *Engaged*. The measured, rich plushness cultivated by Hall was to be found in all his productions of this period: admirably so in *Happy Days* and *No Man's Land* (the latter re-convening, in a new play by Pinter, the world-beating double-act, first seen in David Storey's *Home*, of John Gielgud and Ralph Richardson), but less happily in *Hamlet*, which fell under the curse which has so far damned all National Theatre productions of the play.

There was about Hall's production – formally grouped and symmetrically staged – something fundamentally phlegmatic, which failed to suggest the intellectual excitement at the heart of the piece. Albert Finney, in the title rôle, seemed curiously lacking in vulnerability and consequent mercuriality. Powerful as he was, both physically and intellectually, it was hard to understand why he would hold back for a moment from confronting either Claudius or Gertrude. Despite Finney's natural authority, and the high quality of many of the other leading actors, the company seemed as yet heterogeneous, awkwardly participating in the production rather than embracing it. Just as he had at the RSC, Hall sought a powerful personality to head the acting company, and Finney was his choice to take the company into the new building, whose opening was now imminent. He seemed an admirable choice as company leader, providing continuity with Olivier's régime (and indeed with the Royal Court, a vital influence

John Gielgud and
Ralph Richardson in
No Man's Land, 1975
(Photo: Anthony Crickmay)

Inset: Laurence Olivier
in *The Party*, 1973
(Photo: John Haynes)

which had somewhat faded in recent years), besides being a formidable figure in his own right. Like Olivier, though on a less heroic scale, he was a theatre star, a film star, a stage director and a film director; he had been near the top of Olivier's list to succeed him. In addition to Finney, Hall assembled a group which mingled former RSC actors, actors from the National Theatre Company at the Old Vic, like Denis Quilley, young firebrands from regional theatres (Stephen Rea for example), and the most distinguished actors of Olivier's own generation; he was poised to enter the new building with one of the most powerful acting strengths ever seen on the British stage.

The last play produced at the Old Vic was the symbolically entitled *Watch It Come Down*, a somewhat dubious effort of John Osborne's; but the real farewell to that phase of the National Theatre's history came in the revival, on the very last night the company occupied the building, of *Tribute to the Lady*, Val May's celebration of Lilian Baylis, the creator of the Old Vic. On its first outing, the previous year, Olivier had been the compère; diplomatically pleading ill-health, he now handed the job over to Finney, who despatched his duties with bluff charm. But the evening belonged to that extraordinary generation, including, of course, Olivier, who had learned their craft as classical actors in Baylis's impoverished and chaotically-run playhouse. Heroically and only half-comprehendingly she had kept the great tradition alive, providing a continuous supply of Elizabethan and Jacobean plays for an audience consisting of all classes and all age-groups, as well as a training-ground for young actors: Richardson, Gielgud, Ashcroft (all on stage that night in the Tribute) had become the actors they were at Baylis's Old Vic, as had Michael Redgrave and – a whole generation earlier – Sybil Thorndike, both of whom, desperately frail, were in the audience on that last night of the National Theatre at the Old Vic. In a dazzling assumption, Peggy Ashcroft became Lilian Baylis simply by donning mortar board and gown (one of Baylis's innocent vanities), twisting her mouth (the result of a swimming accident), and adopting the curious, slightly South African, accent in which Baylis had harangued actors, directors, audiences, ministers of the crown and indeed crowned heads of state themselves. "Now you've got to support these boys and girls," Ashcroft hectored her audience, just as Baylis had done, "they work very hard and you have to come to see them even when the play's not as good as it might be. We've got our dear Sybil with us tonight," she went on, and Sybil Thorndike, ninety-four years old, swathed in what appeared to be bales of muslin, turned round in her wheelchair, parked flush against the stage, and cried out "Hello, everybody!" in a voice that shook the theatre to the very Gods. Ralph Richardson spoke irresistibly about Harcourt "Billy" Williams – one-time director of productions – and his passion for Bemax, and John Gielgud tore into "O what a rogue and peasant slave am I!" with astonishing velocity and perfect coherence, providing a moment in which form and content were so perfectly wedded that he seemed to deliver the essence of the play, and the essence of the central tradition of playing Shakespeare, within the three minutes that it took him to speak the speech. The whole evening was an infinitely touching experience, and the presence of so many of Baylis's company on stage and in the auditorium vividly demonstrated the human richness which her theatre had bred, a level of personal generosity and originality which was an inspiration for a subseqent, somehow more pallid, generation. Curiously, Olivier's absence was not strongly felt; the tradition being celebrated here was even older, warmer, and more chaotic than the one that he had transformed into the early years of the National Theatre. Olivier had been a bridge between the hugger-mugger, heart-on-sleeve, innocent procedures of Baylis's Old Vic, and the harsher realities of the modern

Susan Fleetwood and Peggy Ashcroft in *Tribute to the Lady*, 1976 (Photo: Nobby Clark)

Inset: Lilian Baylis (Photo: Angus McBean)

world of the theatre. The presentation of *Tribute to the Lady* was the last night, in fact, not merely of the National Theatre at the Old Vic, but of an entire tradition, a tradition which had to some extent belonged to Peter Brook's category of Poor Theatre, in which the actors and the words had provided the central experience. Lilian Baylis's theatre was motivated by a commitment to the plays and above all to the audience, who developed a personal, an almost familial relationship with the actors and the building. It was a sort of a pact, one it had proved increasingly difficult to maintain. The theatre's lack of funds and its insalubrious location were all part of what it had meant: a theatre where there was no gap between the lives of the audience and the work being done on stage. Hardworking, underpaid people offered up their work to hardworking, underpaid people. It was not a glamorous theatre, not a plump theatre; it was neither escapist nor official; it was direct and vigorous and passionate in its affirmation of the improving power of both great writing and great acting. It had grown directly out of Emma Cons's and Lilian Baylis's Christian faith and their conviction that if you provided audiences with work that was intelligent and inspiring, they would rise to it, and rise above themselves. It was essentially missionary in spirit, neither intellectual nor sophisticated, and it was proudly independent. It was a notion of theatre to which both Sybil Thorndike and Laurence Olivier, both children of clergymen, had subscribed without question. *Tribute to the Lady* was, inevitably, an evening whose tone was profoundly elegiac; Lilian Baylis's Old Vic had no place in the modern world, where the missionary spirit was either suspect or cynically derided, and where, on economic grounds alone, survival without substantial state funding was out of the question for a major theatrical organisation.

The National Theatre on the South Bank was nothing if not that. It had been slowly rising through that last season at the Old Vic, and the scale of the thing took by surprise even those who had seen sketches and models of it. It was positively monolithic. Peter Hall, given a tour of it in 1975, confided in his diary: "a little voice within me still whispers amusedly…perhaps it is already a dodo?" Nonetheless he was the first to see that it was a prominent vouchsafe of the country's commitment to the idea of the theatre. Never in British history had so much money been spent on an artistic venture. Aesthetically, the building reflected the passion of the period for rectilinearity and integrity of materials: the breeze-block, shoe-box idiom whose vogue unfortunately coincided with one of the last great periods of public building; almost all of Britain's unloved new civic theatres were built during these years, the sixties, or in the very early seventies. It was only the unhappy and prolonged difficulties experienced in realising the building that cruelly decreed that it was finally erected nearly ten years after it was designed, when the style it embodied was already *passé* and *démodé*; it was a further misfortune for the building that since it had been designed, its site had been moved from the area in front of the Shell-Mex building to further down-river, to Prince's Meadow, diametrically opposite one of the greatest public buildings in London, Chambers's Somerset House, which gazed serenely, if perhaps with a certain scepticism, on the new building.

Aesthetics, however, were the least of Hall's anxieties in the spring of 1976, when it appeared that the opening would have to be delayed yet again. He boldly insisted on occupying the unfinished building and opening the auditoriums one at a time instead of waiting for completion of the whole; the Lyttelton, the proscenium theatre, the most conventional of the three, opened first. Productions from the Old Vic transferred there; and *Hamlet*, inevitably, was performed on the official First Night. It was clear that the

The new National Theatre
on the South Bank
(Photo: Donald Mill)

46

auditorium was somewhat thankless acoustically, and rather chilling from the point of view of ambience, but the public flocked in. They were particularly appreciative of the public areas of the theatre, the bookstalls and the bars, where music was performed and exhibitions were held and where it was possible to perambulate, gazing down from a great height on one's fellow playgoers, or out across to the North Bank of the Thames, up as far as St Paul's. The openness and airiness of the building, its facilities – restaurants, car parks – and its constant life from ten in the morning to nearly midnight proved to be exactly what the average theatre-goer, frustrated by the tiny bars, the cramped seats and the lack of parking space in West End theatres, had been longing for.

Ralph Richardson, the senior member of the company, spread a kind of wizardly charm over the enterprise, and initiated a tradition which quickly became known as Ralph's Rocket, whereby a firework would be set off for every first night. It was the sort of raffish and personal touch which the building in all its monumentality desperately needed. Alas, the tradition was short-lived and had to be abandoned at the time of the Harrods bomb, when London was more than usually twitchy about terrorist attacks. Nothing was found to replace it. Another manifestation of Richardson's quirky individuality was his invention of what he called Hall's Angels, by which name the motorcycling fraternity within the company were proud to be known, led by the fearless seventy-four year old Harley Davidson fanatic himself, a sort of septuagenarian thespian Evel Knievel. There was a strong need to humanise and properly inhabit the building, which, despite many admirable features such as large and light rehearsal rooms and well-equipped canteens and green rooms, had an inevitably institutional feel to it, with long anonymous corridors, and dressing rooms which had something of the air of the penitentiary about them, looking out as they did onto a concrete courtyard filled with the air-conditioning plant. Character and charm were severely absent, though in most other regards the arrangements were a great advance over what had been available at the Old Vic, and indeed in most theatres in the country. There was a tremendous exhilaration at the gradual inhabitation of the building. Hall's determination to fill the place with active life extended to performing portions of *Tamburlaine The Great* – which had been in rehearsal, in anticipation of the again-delayed opening of the Olivier Theatre, for rather longer, perhaps, than was useful – on the terraces for passers-by, who may have been startled, though agreeably so, to find themselves at very close quarters on the receiving end of Albert Finney's heroic declamation of Marlowe's "mighty line". The production finally opened with some triumph at the Olivier in October of 1976, and theatre-goers were at last able to judge the extraordinary space which Lasdun and his committee of advisors had devised as the largest and most audacious of the auditoriums that formed the National Theatre.

On the whole, they and the critics were impressed, not to say awed, by what they saw, even though much of the elaborate machinery required to make it fully operational had not yet been installed, or was not yet functioning. It was unlike anything else that had ever been created in Britain for the staging of plays, both in scale and in character, a great public space, extrovert and open. The influence was self-evidently Greek, with more than a nod in the direction of the great amphitheatre at Epidauros. Thoughtful observers immediately wondered why this might be so, since no plays of the smallest significance have been written in the English language, or for that matter in any European language, in the form or with the demands of the great Athenian plays of the 4th century BC. As it happens, Marlowe's great epic, which for all its vigorous action, is curiously

Top left: Ralph Richardson lights Ralph's rocket, 1976 (Photo: Tony Russell)

Top right: Michael Bryant, "the nearest thing in the English theatre to a *sociétaire* of the Comédie Française" (Photo: Nobby Clark)

Below: Albert Finney rehearses *Tamburlaine The Great* to an audience of passers-by outside the National, 1976 (Photo: Nobby Clark)

undramatic, proved enormously effective on it; in form it is almost like a pageant, and, apart from Greek dramas of the classical period, pageants, of one sort or another, are what the Olivier Theatre excels at.

Certainly the play chosen for the Royal Gala Opening, that exuberant celebration of village life, Goldoni's *Il Campiello*, detailed, human and realistic, was spectacularly unsuited both to the space and to the occasion, which was above all notable for the somewhat spectral appearance of the man whose name the theatre bore, Laurence Olivier. Frail but commanding, unerringly finding the one place on the stage with absolutely perfect audibility (he had in fact rehearsed on it every morning at 9am for a week), he wished all who worked in the new National Theatre "a sense of the dedication that was once inspired, some years ago, by Lilian Baylis – and others before her...to those who follow, I wish joy eternal of all of it." Denys Lasdun, on taking his seat, was warmly applauded, and Hall and his colleagues braced themselves for the task of simultaneously taming and liberating the space he had designed. The first few years in the new building were an intensive period of trial and error during which the particular character of each auditorium was assessed, its strengths and weaknesses examined, and its possible repertory determined. The last and smallest of the theatres, the Cottesloe, opened the following year; taking advantage of the delay in completing the building, Hall had commissioned an experienced theatre consultant, Iain Mackintosh, to give it as much flexibility as possible within the general proportions and framework of an Elizabethan theatre. It had always been intended as the experimental end of the operation, and this now became eminently possible. It was, in fact, the Cottesloe which found its form first, kicking off with the tremendous event of *Illuminatus!*, Ken Campbell's epic of global paranoia, and continuing with Bill Bryden's staging of Tony Harrison's version of the York Mystery Cycle, with which he and the group of actors he gathered around him established a richly productive style of theatre. Popular without being populist, rooted in a tradition owing nothing to aristocratic patronage or intellectual elaboration, it was earthy, communal and mythic, and its embrace extended to include the American repertory which – often reflecting Hollywood's influence – was a modern equivalent of that tradition, essentially democratic and focused on the lives of ordinary men and women. Bryden's company evolved a playing style which owed a great deal to Northern, including Scottish, traditions, and in keeping with those traditions, music was central, often mingling folk and rock idioms. It was like nothing that had been seen on the British stage, and certainly not the London stage, for some centuries.

The question of style, of character, was unavoidably to the forefront in all the work of the National Theatre – both in itself and in relation to the different auditoriums. Hall had explicitly disassociated himself from the Tynan-Olivier policy of an infinitely adaptable company, reinventing itself for each play; now he had to identify the National Theatre company's own voice. He tried many experiments in forming companies within the company; sometimes they were grouped around a director working in all three auditoriums, sometimes around one of the theatres, playing only in that one. During Hall's régime, companies were grouped around the directors Christopher Morahan, Peter Gill, Bill Gaskill, Peter Wood, Mike Alfreds, Alan Ayckbourn, Michael Bogdanov and Michael Rudman; an attempt to preserve the democratic ideals of the by then defunct Actors' Company was made under the leadership of Ian McKellen and Edward Petherbridge; and loose-knit groups were maintained in both the Olivier and the Lyttelton theatres over a period of some years. The actors who worked together in a

Top: Olivier makes his only appearance on the Olivier stage, at the royal opening of the theatre, October 1976 (Photo: Nobby Clark)

Below left: Part of *The Passion*, the Crucifixion, is performed on the terraces on Easter Sunday, 1977 (Photo: Nobby Clark)

Below right: David Rappaport in *Illuminatus!*, 1977

series of plays staged in the Olivier, for example, from *As You Like It*, through *Amadeus*, *Sisterly Feelings* and *Galileo*, learned to master the particular demands of that theatre (which often meant hitting on the two or three effective parts of the stage and not budging from them), while the parallel group of Lyttelton players learned a thing or two about the harsh and unyielding acoustics of that space. No acting style as such developed, though since intimacy was a virtual impossibility in either theatre, an extrovert and public manner, high in energy and physically dynamic, evolved, somewhat – inevitably – at the expense of nuance and lyricism, though actors of iron lungs and overwhelming charisma like Paul Scofield or Michael Gambon were able to command a sort of operatic full-throatedness which triumphed over the hard walls and long distances of the building.

In the case of individual directors, some, like Ayckbourn or Morahan, simply found a style for each play as they came to it; both might be described as essentially pragmatic in their approach, seeking to realise the author's intentions as faithfully as possible, which resulted in Morahan's case, for example, in an impressive complete *Man and Superman*, and in Ayckbourn's in a production of *A View from the Bridge* which transferred triumphantly to the West End. Others, like Michael Bogdanov, had specific stylistic agendas, which varied in their appropriateness to the work in hand, but which were clear hallmarks of that particular group's work. The work of Peter Wood was always elegant, witty and sophisticated in a manner which recalled Olivier's Old Vic; that of Michael Rudman, while less recognisable in terms of style, often went to the heart of notoriously difficult plays, like *Waiting for Godot* or *Six Characters in Search of an Author*. McKellen and Petherbridge's group was almost by definition committed to the idea of realising the vision of different directors, and gave itself over completely and successfully to, for example, Philip Prowse and Mike Alfreds, two artists with diametrically opposed aesthetics and objectives. In the end, however, it would be hard to say to what degree the group had a character of its own.

Perhaps this was not important. There was no question that once the theatre was in full swing it became remarkably consistent in its level of success. Public demand was high, and awards and accolades showered down on the organisation. In terms of sheer productivity the record was and is impressive. It was as if a whole season or two of West End hit productions had been mounted in the three auditoriums on the South Bank; several of them, indeed, subsequently transferred. But Hall, a man whose artistic conscience was not to be assuaged by mere success, brooded on the theatre's direction.

Clockwise from top:
Michael Gambon, James
Hayes, Michael Thomas,
and Simon Callow in The
Life of Galileo, 1980
(Photo: Zoë Dominic)

Alec McCowen and
John Alderton in
Waiting for Godot, 1987
(Photo: Nobby Clark)

Daniel Massey and
Penelope Wilton in Man
and Superman, 1981
(Photo: Donald Cooper)

Suzan Sylvester and
Michael Gambon in A View
from the Bridge, 1987
(Photo: Nobby Clark)

"I was well on the way to turning the building into a high-class cultural department store," he says in his autobiography. He felt that the National had a very particular mission which went beyond simply providing a high level of what the Arts Council so elegantly describes as "product." In the first few years, simply getting the show on the road was the overwhelming priority. Early on, Hall had survived three crises, the first artistic, the second organisational and the third financial. The artistic crisis was in the form of the unilateral rebellion of one of the associate directors, the brilliantly talented Michael Blakemore, who bridled at the power that Hall wielded in relation to his group of associates. Blakemore resented the lack of consultation in matters of repertory planning and what he felt to be the imposition of a party line on the work of the organisation. Hall was always fearless at taking damage-limiting decisions when he deemed them necessary. If a play was not doing well, it had to leave the repertory; if it looked as if it would be prohibitively expensive, it was shelved. These decisions he made

himself. Hall conceived of the associates as a consultative body, not an executive one; Blakemore preferred the Olivier model, where the associate meetings were a forum for debate in which the artistic director had the casting vote. This was not Hall's way. He had a clear sense of the way the theatre should develop, and it was his job, and that of his team, to make it happen. Blakemore, the disappointed Crown Prince of the Olivier years, was not content to serve the will of a man with whom his relationship, dating back to his early years as an actor at pre-RSC Stratford, had never been easy. After an abortive press scandal worked up by his friends, Blakemore resigned and never worked at Hall's National Theatre again. Miller, too, had quietly phased himself out of the National, but despite the continuing presence of Peter Wood as an associate (who had anyway worked as much for the RSC as he had for Olivier's National Theatre) and the occasional return of John Dexter – never officially an associate under Hall – it was Blakemore's stormy departure which symbolised the breaking of the last link with the Olivier period.

On the whole, Hall's relationship with his associates was easy and supportive; they formed a loose but unified team. The group had little in common beyond the fact that Hall admired them: John Bury had been his Head of Design at the RSC, as John Goodwin had been Head of Press and Publications there. Michael Kustow, who had created Theatre-Go-Round, the RSC's touring group, was now head of all ancillary events at the National. Harrison Birtwistle as Head of Music was an astonishingly bold and fruitful appointment, while the Head of the Literary Department, John Russell Brown, was a figure as far removed from Kenneth Tynan or any potential Tynanism as could be conceived of. He was almost equally far removed from John Barton, who had had such a liberating effect on Hall's creativity at the RSC. Brown was an academic through and through and his theory of Free Shakespeare – Shakespeare unadorned by interpretation – may have led to a certain stolidity and sobriety in Hall's Shakespeare productions in the earlier part of his régime at the National; he showed little flair for commissioning new plays, or for introducing foreign ones. Brown left to take up an American academic appointment halfway through Hall's period, and the arrival of the writer and director Nicholas Wright as Literary Manager brought in a period of great expansion. After Blakemore, there was no palace revolt; there was no need for one.

Hall's second crisis – in 1979 – was industrial, and his handling of it was certain too, and remarkably brave, considering not only the prevailing climate of industrial relations, but also that he was in the midst of trying to open both a major production of his own and a vast and recalcitrant new complex. The two strikes, the first more of a skirmish, were a test of will, and Hall – a lifelong Labour voter – risked the opprobrium not only of the union but of his natural supporters by defying them. He went so far as to continue to operate the theatres without the stage staff, playing shows on sets belonging to other shows, with limited light and limited sound, until finally the strike dribbled to a halt, and the building resumed its proper working. It was a moment of great psychological importance in the history of the National Theatre. Not merely did it establish – always a matter of dispute in labour-intensive organisations – who was in control, it galvanised the whole company, which had glumly endured the demoralising failure of the building to open on time. The Battle of Britain spirit, apparently indispensable to these operations, finally emerged and the refusal to be bullied by a single group within the organisation made the company pull together in a very positive way. The building, and the physical running of it, were not going to be allowed to dominate the work of putting on plays. The strike was a useful reminder of that vital priority.

Peter Hall, 1988
(Photo: John Haynes)

Hall's third crisis was financial, and led, in 1985, to the temporary closure of the Cottesloe theatre (a highly visible protest, given the unflagging vitality of its work) then to his mobilisation of the heads of regional theatre behind his impassioned assault – delivered from on top of a coffee-table – on the inadequacies of government funding and Arts Council management. This act of leadership had the very useful side-effect of removing the National Theatre from the suspicion of seeming to be a fat cat creaming off the bulk of the Arts Council budget at the expense of everyone else. Hall's calculated outburst – a phrase which is something of a pleonasm, since little that Hall did, however deeply felt, was not calculated – placed the National at the head of the nation's theatre, which is precisely where it should have been from the beginning. It also succeeded in its primary purpose, which was to shame the government into increasing the revenue grant. The Cottesloe was open again within six months. Hall's strength in a crisis was the salvation of the National Theatre, at a time when there were mutterings from the increasingly bullish Thatcher administration that perhaps after all the state had no business bailing out the arts. Few people could have brought to bear the weight and the passion in the cause of the arts that Hall mustered over those years. He seemed to thrive on it, though the strain of being active on so many fronts began subtly to undermine his health, as it had Olivier's: throughout the rehearsals of *Amadeus*, for example, he was receiving laser-beam treatment for a painful eye condition. Temperamentally, though, he was well adapted to crisis; as Peter Wood acutely remarked of him, "the moment a crisis occurred, his whole being went into a state of relaxation." An insomniac, he put to use more hours of the day than might be considered humanly possible; if there was a fault, it was in over-extension of himself, both within the organisation and outside it.

Everything that Hall did was highly visible, whether selling wallpaper (the notorious "very Peter Hall, very Sandersons" advertising campaign) or fronting the television arts programme, *Aquarius*. He was very frank about his need for money, which sometimes gave an unattractive impression of mercenariness, though few people denied that the remuneration offered the director of the National Theatre was risible by comparison with that of the head of any other nationalised industry, or indeed with what he might have earned in the commercial sector. Aspersions were also cast on his ability to be in so many places at once. Some of his productions had a routine quality to them, but nonetheless his work as a director was central to the whole output of the National Theatre in his time, just as Olivier's work as an actor had been central during his. The notion, occasionally mooted, of a non-creative *Intendant* on the German model has never seemed a good option; a director who is involved in the grubby, ambitious, naked business of getting work onto the stage has a much greater chance of uniting his colleagues engaged in the same activity. At any one time, they could be up to seven hundred and fifty in number at the National Theatre on the South Bank, so the personal touch, as attempted, with considerable success, by Olivier, was more elusive for Hall or for his successors – to remember the names of even the acting company was virtually impossible for one person. But the man made himself highly accessible to those who approached him, and a new member of the company, as I was in 1979, was able from time to time to spend an hour or so with him in his office, under the portrait of Bruckner which was his inspiration, discussing my problems and hopes. But it was not one-way; as often as not we would end up discussing *his* problems and hopes. His curious combination of authority and vulnerability, of conviction and self-doubt, of political calculation and unaffected love of the theatre, were evidently the source of all his work. He was a formidable operator, and

Simon Callow and Paul Scofield in *Amadeus*, 1979 (Photo: Nobby Clark)

you had to be on your toes with him at all times; but he was also touchingly human, riven with uncertainty about his own gifts and seeking security in the strength of his organisation, all the while longing to get back onto the rehearsal room floor to have another go, to get it right this time. A lot of all of this he laid bare, as no theatre director had ever done before him, in his *Diaries*, bringing out another contradiction in this complex man: passionately defensive of his private life, he recklessly exposed himself and others, at the cost of friendships, famously, for example, with Harold Pinter (temporarily, as it turned out). In a sense, the *Diaries* better deserved the title he chose for his slightly less revealing autobiography: *Making An Exhibition Of Myself.*

If his classical productions from the seventies seemed somehow stolid, lacking the passion that he undoubtedly felt for the plays, his Pinter productions set the standard, directed with acute awareness of the music in the language and the pressure inside the situations. With *Amadeus*, a play whose text was a foaming Niagara of rhetoric and theatrical gesture on which great ideas bobbed along like tiny barks, he felt liberated from any excessive reverence for the punctuation, and showed that he was as capable as anyone of serving up sumptuous spectacle and thrilling *coups de théâtre*, the Barnum and Bailey side of him which he generally suppressed, but which was brilliantly effective. *Amadeus* proved a number of things: that Shaffer's theatrical genius was not the invention of John Dexter; that the public was longing for big plays which dealt with big themes in a generous and passionate manner; and that the Olivier auditorium could be one of the great theatrical spaces in the world, given the right play and the right production. Hall went much further into the possibilities of that space with *The Oresteia*, perhaps his single most adventurous and most completely realised production for the National Theatre, and one of the key productions of the post-war period, an overwhelming renewal of our contact with the roots of drama, drama as a collective act of remembering and affirming, and of course perfectly suited to Lasdun's vast amphitheatre. Nothing so thorough-going in the use of masks had been attempted on this scale; the power and the purity released by the production were startling. Tony Harrison's text had created a language, both recognisable and comprehensible but also utterly other, primitive and primal, which stirred deep ancestral memories.

Animal Farm was a modern experiment along the same lines, almost equally stirring and resonant; but Hall and the National Theatre came a real cropper with an attempt to make a musical out of the strange and terrible life story of the actress Jean Seberg. It was an unusual instance of the values of the director and indeed of the organisation being subverted by another altogether more ruthless and savage will: that of the Broadway musical machine. Hall had been attracted by the material – with its book by Julian Barry, lyrics by Christopher Adler and music by Marvin Hamlisch – as well, no doubt, as by the perfectly honourable expectation that he might make a little money for the National Theatre and, eventually, himself. Wisely, he decided on a preliminary workshop period, under his supervision, which yielded a dazzling showing, tightly and wittily choreographed by Stuart Hopps, brilliantly and harrowingly performed by a very young Kelly Hunter as Seberg and Shaun Curry as Romain Gary. The packed and highly discriminating audience in the rehearsal room in which the result of the workshop was performed had no doubt that the National Theatre had, given only a small amount of re-writing and refocussing, a great hit on its hands. There was the added excitement of seeing an exceptional new talent – Kelly Hunter's – revealed for the first time in all its splendour. The show was macabre and mordant, exhilarating in its energy and fearless in

Top: Kelly Hunter and John Savident in *Jean Seberg*, 1983 (Photo: Nobby Clark)

Below: Barrie Rutter, Karl Johnson and Gorden Kaye in *Animal Farm* in 1985 when it transferred to the Lyttelton (Photo: Nobby Clark)

probing a very dark and disturbed psyche and the forces that had created it. How then was it that the *Jean Seberg* that actually appeared on the stage of the Olivier Theatre was such a lame and gormless experience? Essentially, the familiar Broadway paranoia had taken possession of the project, and the time-honoured remedy of blood-letting was invoked. The choreographer and the leading man were both changed, the book was softened and sentimentalised, the music became more formulaic. From being an examination of the destructive forces within Seberg and the pressures applied from without – a highly political and critical allegory – it became another sad show-biz story which seemed to have no place whatever on the stage of the National Theatre. Even Kelly Hunter at the centre of it all seemed strangely subdued. Loss of control of that sort was quite untypical of Hall. There was nothing inherently wrong in the notion of what is inevitably essentially a classical company tackling the musical genre; on the contrary, it was exactly what such a company should be tackling, endlessly expanding its range and its skills. Mounting *Guys and Dolls* had been Olivier's most cherished dream, and its cancellation by the Board had been the final blow, he maintained, that broke his spirit.

When the company did eventually tackle the piece, in Richard Eyre's joyous 1982 production, it proved to be one of the crowning glories of Hall's régime, and immediately suggested that Eyre would be a contender for the succession. The man whose range encompassed this production as well as Trevor Griffiths's *Comedians* (which had played at the Old Vic during the National Theatre's last year there) and a series of remarkable productions at the Nottingham Playhouse, which he had made the most eminent and enterprising of all Britain's regional theatres, clearly had many of the qualities required of the director of the National Theatre, and Eyre swiftly became an associate director of the company. The succession was smoothly and somehow inevitably effected in 1988, with none of the sub-Shakespearean shenanigans which had heralded Hall's régime. Hall himself ended his time at the National Theatre as he had begun it: with a production of *The Tempest* in a cycle of Late Plays which also consisted of *Cymbeline* and *The Winter's Tale*. But this *Tempest* was radically different from the one which he had directed at the Old Vic, with John Gielgud expressing the dramatist's valediction in his inimitably elegiac tones. Now, in 1988, Hall saw the play as a swift and savage revenge drama with a harsh and embittered Prospero at its centre. The part was played by that remarkable actor, Michael Bryant, the nearest thing in the English Theatre to a *sociétaire* in the manner of the Comédie Française, an actor who had simply decided at a certain point that he wanted to remain at the National Theatre for the rest of his working life, and who had illuminated part after part, large and small, supporting and leading, cameo or virtuoso. His Brand, Jaques, and Enobarbus, to name a tiny handful of his parts with the company, were all remarkable in performance and new in conception. His Prospero was white-hot and full of inner violence, an unforgettable reclamation of a part which can seem curiously one-dimensional; and Hall's production was remarkably vigorous.

The Late Plays had opened in the Cottesloe Theatre, and the directness and swift-moving energy of the productions derived to a large extent from the intimacy and fluidity of that space; the dynamism was retained when the productions moved to the Olivier. Like most of the resident directors at the National, Hall had come to prefer the Cottesloe over both the other auditoriums, even for epic work like the plays of Shakespeare or Lope de Vega. He himself had evolved astonishingly and daringly as a director during his tenure, opening up large areas of exploration, from the Greeks to literary adaptation (the Orwell), on to experimental Shakespeare – *Coriolanus* with the audience on stage and the

Top: Jimmy Jewel and Jonathan Pryce in *Comedians*, 1975 (Photo: Gerald Murray)

Below: Barrie Rutter, Bob Hoskins and David Healy in *Guys and Dolls*, 1982 (Photo: John Haynes)

Late Plays in their unified settings. One of his most remarkable productions was the virtually forgotten *Martine* by French playwright Jean-Jacques Bernard, in which Hall revealed his profound passion for the bucolic, and his willingness to explore almost forgotten repertory.

In fact, the repertory in Hall's time was vast, with the constant rediscovery and sometimes re-invention of little-known writers: Horváth, Schnitzler, Nestroy. Especially after Nicholas Wright's appointment as Literary Manager, the National Theatre's record in staging new writing was exemplary. As well as the continuing support of mainstream dramatists like Ayckbourn, Stoppard and Shaffer, the generation of Royal Court writers of the sixties and seventies – Bond, Brenton, Hare – was given access to all three auditoriums, placing them firmly in the forefront of the great public debate that Tynan had wistfully dreamed of, but which Hall achieved. He encouraged a generation of writers to speak for England and created a body of work that shows every sign of providing a durable account of what it was like to be alive in the 1980s. The full resources of the National Theatre, now increasingly efficient from the technical point of view, were made available to these writers so that what they had to say should be given the greatest possible chance of reaching the public. In this sense, Hall's National Theatre was far more of a public forum than Olivier's had ever been; there was a tremendous confidence about the right and indeed the duty of the organisation to make a contribution to the life of the country. Big targets were unsparingly hit; *Pravda* was the high-point of this great social venture.

The establishment did not always take it lying down. Like Olivier, Hall had his scandal – Howard Brenton's *The Romans in Britain* – one of the more farcical episodes in the relationship of the press and the National Theatre, where an entirely symbolic male rape in an allegorical play examining Britain's relationship with Northern Ireland was denounced by Mary Whitehouse and the tabloid press as an exercise in sexual titillation. Although there was a great deal of hysteria and an aborted criminal prosecution before the whole thing faded away, the episode really demonstrated Hall's complete command of his own Board. There was no vestige of Olivier's anxious kow-towing to Chandos; Hall was, to put it mildly, not the Board's creature. In Stratford, he had worked from the beginning in close cahoots with its chairman Fordham Flower, making him an ally rather than an adversary; now, with the National Theatre Board on the South Bank, he marshalled them behind him on a matter which was, in fact, considerably more controversial than the scandal that had surrounded *Soldiers*, which even at the time had a feeling of ashes being raked over, of old men's battles being fought again. Hall's political astuteness ensured that power resided firmly with him. The Board, like the associates, were there to help to realise the programme, not to determine it.

Smaller experimental work, too, was encouraged with the formation of a Studio under that gentle but insistent explorer, Peter Gill. Michael Kustow's Platform Performances, three-quarter hour pre-show events on the stages of the three theatres, allowed actors to explore byways of the dramatic repertory, or the medium of public verse-speaking, like the complete Sonnets of Shakespeare or Auden's *Letter to Lord Byron*; there was a forum, too, for practitioners to discuss their work with the public. Meanwhile, Nicholas Wright had initiated a particularly fruitful series of commissions, translations and adaptations. The band of directors who regularly worked at the National Theatre all did fine work over Hall's period; they included fiery visits from John Dexter, a sort of RSM of the theatre, always bent on training his actors into a crack unit, and generally trying to

Clockwise from top left:
Wendy Morgan in *Martine*, 1985
(Photo: John Haynes)

Anthony Hopkins in *Pravda*, 1985
(Photo: Nobby Clark)

Greg Hicks (*centre*) in *The Romans in Britain*, 1980
(Photo: Laurence Burns)

Simon Callow speaking the complete Sonnets of Shakespeare as a Platform performance, 1980
(Photo: Michael Mayhew)

foment palace revolution. It was noticeable that, in sharp contrast to Olivier's time, foreign directors were rarely invited to work with the company; indeed, the only one was Maximilian Schell who directed a brilliantly organised and physically exciting production of Horváth's *Tales from the Vienna Woods*. There is little question that the company would have gained from contact with directors from different theatrical traditions, but a decision, conscious or not, had clearly been made to encourage a specifically indigenous acting style.

The whole question of the development of the company remained vexed. In a group as large as that required to fill the stages of Lasdun's great theatrical warehouse on the South Bank a certain amorphousness was inevitable. It was increasingly hard to focus on the development of individual actors, and to nurture their work through a series of productions. With very rare exceptions – Brenda Blethyn, for example, whose brilliant talent declared itself in time-honoured fashion when she went on in *Tales from the Vienna Woods* as an understudy and then took over the part; and Imelda Staunton, who accomplished a similar leap by taking over as Miss Adelaide in *Guys and Dolls* – actors tended to leave the company at the same level at which they had entered it. Moreover, there was no training structure within the company: no acting classes, no classes in special skills, no regular and systematic vocal or physical training. Tynan's Acting Gymnasium remained unopened. Hall had unsuccessfully tried to interest John Gielgud in holding master-classes in the performance of *The Importance of Being Earnest*, which might have provided a pattern for an immensely rewarding line of work: direct example is lamentably underrated as a didactic method, and can impart an understanding of certain essentials in a way that no theoretical teaching can quite manage. Craft-training was only available if it was required for the needs of a particular production: Hall's work with masks for *The Oresteia*, for instance, was searching and radically instructive to the actors who took part in it, and influenced their work in very different sorts of plays, but the experiment ended with the show. It may be that there is something in the English tradition, so essentially pragmatic, which believes that the training of an actor should be strictly confined to Drama School, and that anything more should be acquired entirely by practical experience. In effect, this means that individual directors pass on their practices: people as different as Michael Bogdanov and Mike Alfreds introduced their companies to a bewildering array of rehearsal techniques which were sometimes endured rather than embraced.

As for the composition of the company, more or less every actor of distinction in the British Isles has appeared with it at one time or another; a star actor generally joins the National Theatre for two or three plays, and to some extent that actor will help to create the group's sense of identity. This was certainly true of Ian McKellen, for example, with his extrovert and romantic personality, or John Wood, with his electric neurotic intensity. But it was very hard for the company to establish an organic identity apart, that is, from Bryden's group at the Cottesloe, whose roughness sometimes developed into mere anarchy, but which was nevertheless always identifiable and almost always invigorating (bringing out for example usually submerged folkloric qualities in *A Midsummer Night's Dream*, in which they were magisterially joined by Paul Scofield and Susan Fleetwood, casting which was almost metaphorical, the divine ones joining the rude mechanicals). It seems that, in the absence of an attached Drama School (as at the Comédie Française) or any all-informing theory of acting (as at the Moscow Art Theatre or the Berliner Ensemble), the National Theatre will always proceed with this informal association of

Top: Greg Hicks (*centre*) as Orestes, with the Chorus of Furies in *The Oresteia*, 1981

Below: Peter Hall rehearsing with the Chorus of Old Men (Photos: Nobby Clark)

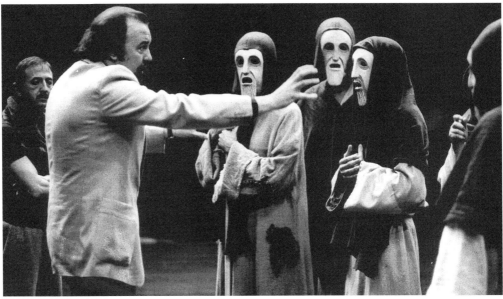

talent. It has obvious gains, and often companies of extraordinarily high levels of accomplishment have been assembled for a few months at a time, achieving great feats of collective brilliance – brilliance rather than depth. It is disappointing that neither of our great companies is able to produce work with the many-layered intensity of, for example, Ingmar Bergman's Royal Dramatic Theatre, Lev Dodin's Maly Theatre or Yevgeny Arye's Gesher. That work comes about because of the conditions in which it is rehearsed, with a fiercely applied methodology evolved from the drama training which all its artists have undergone, and from which they have derived, at the very least, a common language. Sometimes, as far as understanding each other's method is concerned, English groups function in a positive Babel. It might be interesting to explore the notion of a drama school attached to the company, either by absorbing one of the existing schools, or by creating a new one with the specific purpose of training the sort of actor that the company wishes to encourage. As far as the ideal of the ensemble is concerned, it is interesting to note that Hall, after a period of West End work in association with the producer Bill Kenwright, returned to the Old Vic in 1997 to form a company based on repertory principles, with the declared aim of across-the-board depth of casting and evolution of company playing. But, as usual in the British Theatre, he did so on a virtual shoe-string, as if he were some obstinate eccentric being allowed to indulge his caprice, as long as it doesn't cost anything. Indeed, the money for Hall's Company at the Old Vic has come from no British source, but from those Torontonian theatrical Maecenases, the Mirvishes, *père et fils* who have finally, at the time of writing decided to unburden themselves of the building, which is up for sale. Whether Hall will find the money or the energy to continue his highly successful experiment remains to be seen. He richly deserves to.

Hall had left the National Theatre with its position at the centre of British theatrical life assured. His relations with the Board had been equable, though Max Rayne, who resigned from the chairmanship at the same time as the changeover of director, managed a parting firework just before he left in 1988: he had secured the Royal patent for the theatre, which would henceforth be known as the Royal National Theatre. This gesture was festively intended, no doubt, but its unilateral nature – Rayne had consulted no one at all – was not warmly appreciated by those immediately affected by the change, namely the organisation itself. There was considerable doubt as to its value, or indeed its point. It would, the argument ran, make the theatre more attractive when it attempted international tours; it was, too, an endorsement of the achievements of the last 25 years. But the historic name of National Theatre, embodying 150 years of dreams, and now two remarkable periods of theatrical activity under its banner, was thought to be its own endorsement; moreover the implicit twinning with the Royal Shakespeare Company was one which neither organisation wished to encourage. The royalness of the National Theatre has been somewhat muted: if not exactly played down, it has hardly been fanfared, either, and created a moment of comic awkwardness when one of the first productions of Eyre's régime, *Single Spies* by Alan Bennett, seemed to be taking the patent over-literally, in the famous scene (in the second play of the two plays, *A Question of Attribution)*, featuring Her Majesty in conversation with Anthony Blunt. The tabloid press became hysterical for a day or two, smuggling cameras with tele-photo lenses into the auditorium for a glimpse of Prunella Scales's uncannily accurate HMQ. This was Eyre's Scandal, a very merry affair by comparison with his predecessors'; there was no royal visit to the play, but no one ended up in the Tower, either.

Clockwise from top left:
Prunella Scales and Alan Bennett in *A Question of Attribution*, 1988
(Photo: John Haynes)

Steven Mackintosh, Geraldine James, and Jeremy Flynn in *Cymbeline*, 1988
(Photo: John Haynes)

Laurence Olivier arrives at the Stage Door for a performance to celebrate his 80th birthday, 1987. Peter Hall and Richard Eyre at right
(Photo: Nobby Clark)

Richard Eyre:
Consolidator

Richard Eyre inherited an organisation in extraordinarily good shape, and one with which he was thoroughly familiar. He had been an associate director since 1982; he had directed plays with considerable success in each auditorium, and was acutely aware, from the beginning of his régime, of their shortcomings. Alone of the three Directors of the National Theatre, he had had no part in designing the building, and was frank in his acknowledgement of the difficulties created by the incompetence of some aspects of the design, above all in the matter of acoustics. The Cottesloe Theatre, installed by Iain Mackintosh and his associates, was exempt from these strictures; but both the Olivier and the Lyttelton posed huge problems, the latter having a particularly intractable acoustic, forcing actors and directors to play as much of the action as possible downstage, and facing out. And the Lyttelton is a relatively small auditorium. Perfunctory in its design – all the imaginative energy seemed to have gone into the Olivier – it has the feel of a much larger theatre, with none of the intimacy generally possessed by proscenium arch theatres. From the beginning of his time at the National, Eyre has concerned himself with humanising and customising the auditoriums. A man of a very different cast from Peter Hall – more constitutional monarch, perhaps, than emperor – he is every bit as committed as his predecessor to the function of the theatre in helping to maintain the central values of social life, and its indispensible role as the sounding board of society, but he is less engaged with the Epic than Hall; and all three auditoriums at the National Theatre are to some extent inherently epic. Eyre has contrived to work against this from the beginning.

Elegant, ironic, razor-keen in intellect, he is an observer (a writer, incidentally, of exceptional distinction) and a celebrator. It is as impossible to imagine Richard Eyre's production of *The Oresteia* as it would be to envisage Hall's of *Guys and Dolls*; equally Hall's Tennessee Williams, lush and operatic, is radically different from Eyre's leaner, more lyrical conception of the same writer. Eyre values lucidity over everything; Hall is in the business of telling myths, whether by Aeschylus or Pinter, Orwell or Marvin Hamlisch. Eyre has expressed his plan for the National Theatre in characteristically sharp terms: essentially he believes that the theatre must, above all, be theatrical. The uniqueness of the medium is what he has sought to stress: what can only be performed in a theatre. "Theatre only ever exists in the present tense," he has written. "Theatre depends on the relationship of a performer to a group of spectators, and to the disposition of mankind to tell each other stories." Above all, that means contact between the performers and their audiences, and preserving "the scale of the human figure and the human voice." Where Hall talks of myth, Eyre speaks of metaphor: "a room becomes a world, a group of characters become the whole society." He believes that theatre is where human beings talk to each other at their most lucid and forceful.

Though neither Eyre nor Hall has sought to impose his taste on his colleagues, inevitably their personalities and enthusiasms have had a fundamental influence on the overall tone of the building. Eyre's unceasing diligence and his total commitment to the National Theatre (he has scarcely worked for anyone else during his whole time in the job), wooing sponsors, working punishing hours in the office and on the rehearsal floor, not to mention his ability to make personal contact with the entire staff of the organisation, almost all of whom, by some supernatural feat, he does seem to know by name, has created a particularly productive mood in the organisation. His choice of associate directors has mirrored his own style. The linearity and good taste of his work are matched by those of, for example, Howard Davies and Nicholas Hytner, both of

Richard Eyre
(Photo: John Haynes)

whom share a certain coolness and irony with him; but perhaps his key associate has been the writer-director David Hare. Eyre's production of Hare's State-of-the-Nation trilogy (*Racing Demon, Murmuring Judges, The Absence of War*) was perhaps the central achievement of his régime, as well as his greatest personal triumph, engaging directly and with brilliant theatrical vividness with key issues of modern life in this country; not for nothing was Eyre once head of BBC TV's *Play for Today*. Hare's theatrical Anatomy of Britain was just that: a play utterly of and for today, and the Olivier Theatre was packed to bursting point when the trilogy was performed together on a single day. Hare's continuing growth as a dramatist has been remarkable, and it has all happened within the National Theatre; his mission, impassioned but always witty, to test the idea of goodness, whether in personal or political terms, has yielded play after play of increasing emotional intensity and eloquence. The precision and the passion are exactly matched in Eyre's work, and in his leadership, but there is an unexpected carnival side to his personality, at its most unbuttoned in *Guys and Dolls*. The production was revived at the end of his tenure in 1996/97 with equal, if not greater, success than on its first outing. Just as before, it fulfilled the same twin purposes of providing the company with an opportunity to display its collective versatility, and sustaining the theatre's always perilous financial health – a perpetual objective in a theatre which by its very charter must from time to time explore unknown theatrical territories into which all of its audience will not always be willing to follow it.In *Utopia and Other Places*, Eyre writes that "composing the content of the repertoire is always a delicate balancing act between adventure and caution, between known classics and the unknown, recent plays and new ones, but the spine of the work will always be the classics. They are our genetic link with the past and our means of decoding the present...the problem anyone running a theatre faces is that there are a finite number of classics, and many of them rotate in the repertory of our large companies." His solution to this problem has been two-fold. First came the exploration of a genre with its own classics, hitherto little explored by the National, that of the musical. Having, in the opinion of many, come of age in the 70s and 80s – though there is a lively dissenting view which maintains that tunes and terpsichore are the proper Dionysian province of musical comedy – the musical theatre became a central part of the repertory. No new musicals were attempted (perhaps the memory of *Jean Seberg* and the dread example of the RSC's *Carrie* and *Poppy* were too daunting), but there was a steady flow of productions of the works of Stephen Sondheim, all gaining from the strength of the available acting resources, if sometimes losing from the musical point of view. There were also striking revivals of two very grown-up musicals: *Carousel* and *Lady in the Dark*. Eyre's second solution to the problem of staleness in the repertory was to seek innovative approaches to classical production. He himself has had a sometimes unhappy time with that particular repertory: in common with his predecessors, he was defeated by *Hamlet*. Like Hall, and for that matter Olivier (though Olivier's was on film), he had had an earlier success with a radical production of the same play (at the Royal Court with Jonathan Pryce's sardonic Prince, literally possessed, *Exorcist*-like, by demons). When he came to do it again, however, in – as it were – the Official Version, it became dutiful. His Hamlet, Daniel Day-Lewis, was wrestling with his own personal demons at the time, and they eventually proved too powerful for him; his successor in the rôle, Ian Charleson, in the grip of full-blown AIDS, heroically playing the part as his life literally ebbed away from him, brought an intensity that people who saw it can never erase from their memories, and which put the plague of the age, the terrifying virus which was visibly

The David Hare Trilogy, 1993 – clockwise: Robin Bailey and John Thaw in The Absence of War

Michael Bryant and Richard Pasco in Murmuring Judges

Richard Pasco and Oliver Ford Davies in Racing Demon (Photos: John Haynes)

consuming him, centre stage in the most graphic way conceivable. This Hamlet, in a way that is given to few theatre performances, transcended its circumstances, transcended the theatre itself, and became not a representation but a reality.

Eyre's *Macbeth*, his *Changeling* and his *Bartholomew Fair* were none of them entirely successful, largely due to the problems associated with their auditoriums. He scored a bulls-eye, however, with *Richard III* in the Lyttelton, which, by a brilliant transposition of period became very much a Play For Today, with McKellen's Mosley-like, only slightly scoliotic Crookback, a frighteningly credible dictator in the making. And he had another in 1997, at the end of his time at the head of the company, with a *King Lear* (in the Cottesloe) in which Ian Holm returned triumphantly after a long absence to the playwright in whose work he had done such extraordinary work for so many years with Hall's RSC. Other directors' productions of Shakespeare in Eyre's time were often quirky and somehow off-kilter. Deborah Warner's *Lear* with Brian Cox, Phyllida Lloyd's *Pericles*, Robert Lepage's *A Midsummer Night's Dream*, all failed to deliver the plays with full force. Partly this was a question of the looseness of the companies assembled; frequently they were ad hoc groups, who had had no experience of playing together and often very little experience of playing Shakespeare at all. But very often it was a result of an attempt at a radical reconception of the plays which had its origins in visual imagery rather than in textual concerns, or even in psychological verisimilitude.

Paradoxically, Eyre, the champion of lucidity, was the driving force behind this stress on the non-verbal. Admitting that he had once been less visually aware than he might have been, he had since undergone a Pauline conversion; now he went on record as saying that he would rather a play were over- than under-designed. Undoubtedly this conviction owed a great deal to his experience with the National Theatre's auditoriums. A tendency developed, in the Olivier Theatre, of filling the stage with as much scenery as possible to tame its chilly, wide-open spaces; Eyre's production of *The Government Inspector*, designed by John Gunter, accordingly took place on a vast mound of bureaucratic paraphernalia, filing cabinets, desks and literal mountains of paperwork. It was a staggering spectacle, but it left the play with nowhere to go. This school of design, a sort of secular, unneurotic Expressionism, became very familiar on the larger stages of the National Theatre; in the Lyttelton it was further informed by the need to bring the action as close as possible to the front. Eyre's *Changeling* actually spilled over the lip of the stage. One of the most successful productions in the National's history, the startling reclamation of JB Priestley's *An Inspector Calls* by Stephen Daldry and his designer Ian McNeil, was as visually audacious as anything ever seen on the South Bank, but the visual excitement was informed and inspired by unmistakable moral passion. The same team's *Machinal*, by contrast, seemed a celebration of theatre technology and a relentless physicalisation of the play's every element, to the ultimate detriment of the work itself.

It was the conviction that the visual dimension was crucial that led to a strong tendency to approach directors with a performance art background, or with a highly advanced visual sense. Declan Donnellan, who always works in close association with his designer Nick Ormerod; Simon McBurney of Theatre de Complicite; Matthew Warchus. The choreographer-director Martha Clarke staged an only partially successful *Alice's Adventures Under Ground*; and the National became Robert Lepage's London home, demonstrating his marvels of technological poetry. Meanwhile, more conventionally-orientated directors continued to produce traditional stagings, and amongst this work were plays which performed excellently at the box office, often transferring or touring

Ian McKellen in
Richard III, 1990
(Photo: John Haynes)

72

abroad: *Single Spies* by Alan Bennett, directed by the author; his adaptation of *The Wind in the Willows*, directed by Nicholas Hytner, who also staged Bennett's *The Madness of George III*; Arthur Miller's *Broken Glass*, directed by David Thacker; Cocteau's *Les Parents Terribles*, directed by Sean Mathias, which became *Indiscretions* on Broadway; and *Dealer's Choice*, by Patrick Marber, who also directed the play.

There was a determination to integrate the work of ethnically-based companies, like Tara Arts, into the mainstream; the Studio continued to facilitate the development of inexperienced dramatists and to become something very like the Writers' School of Olivier's dreams, with residencies in Johannesburg, Edinburgh and Lithuania. The Platform Performances at the same time became less of an experimental crucible and focused more on discussion encounters between the audience and theatre practitioners and writers in general; while the company's encouragement of living dramatists remained committed and diverse, from seasoned writers like Stoppard, Edgar, and Bennett, to then almost-unknowns like Patrick Marber and Martin McDonagh. It is of course true that any theatre's policy must be exclusive to some degree, and extraordinary writers like Peter Barnes and David Rudkin, whose work had earlier been championed by the RSC, failed to achieve productions at the National Theatre, and in the absence of any other organisation large enough to undertake their ambitious works, effectively fell silent. Nonetheless, the range of new work undertaken during Eyre's period is broadly representative of nearly every strand in new English-language writing today, and the percentage of new work among the theatre's successes is exceptionally high. Hare's Trilogy, his *Skylight*, Bennett's *Single Spies* and *Madness of George III*, Stoppard's *Arcadia*, Gems's *Stanley*, Gill's *Cardiff East*, McDonagh's *The Cripple of Inishmaan*, and, one of the most potent productions of the decade, Tony Kushner's two-part epic *Angels in America*, as much as anything else in the repertory, are what will be recalled from Eyre's time at the National Theatre.

A significant number of those plays appeared at the Cottesloe, which continued to be the most flexible and the most communicative of the three venues. It is mildly ironic that it was the name of the decent, tenacious Lord Cottesloe, Chairman of the Arts Council and facilitator of the funding of the building, which should have been most affectionately evoked, while the names of the two formidable men who brought the National Theatre into being, Laurence Olivier and Oliver Lyttelton, often came attached with a derogatory epithet. Richard Eyre became increasingly determined to do something about the shortcomings of these two auditoriums, and at the very end of his time at the National Theatre he instigated alterations in the Olivier which enabled it to be transformed into a theatre-in-the-round, should the need arise. Acoustical adjustments were installed in both the Olivier and the Lyttelton. The building in general needed attention, too. In common with many other constructions of the period, the National Theatre had failed to improve with age. Rather surprisingly, it had become a Grade Two listed building, and Lasdun himself fiercely resisted any attempt to alter his work. He had had unprecedented rights within the building: for ten years after the opening he had had the power of veto over any design which spilled over the parameters of the Olivier stage into the auditorium, and he and an influential group of architectural journalists passionately defended the appearance of the building itself. But it was unarguable that the concrete which he had chosen as the basic element of his conception, inside and outside, had weathered very poorly. Coming into its own at night, with the great flying towers dramatically lit to resemble the mythic scene sketches of Edward Gordon Craig, by day

Clockwise from top left:
Griff Rhys Jones in *The Wind in the Willows*, 1990
(Photo: Clive Barda)

Nigel Hawthorne in *The Madness of George III*, 1991
(Photo: Donald Cooper)

Nicholas Day, Tom Georgeson and David Bark-Jones in *Dealer's Choice*, 1995
(Photo: Hugo Glendinning)

Sheila Gish in *Les Parents Terribles*, 1994
(Photo: Mark Douet)

its massive slabs and drab blotchy surfaces seem at best functional, at worst anonymously oppressive. The public areas in the foyers, one of the principal successes of the whole scheme, needed expansion, while the areas outside the theatre on the embankment had become shabby, partly as a result of the presence of a small parking lot and a large garbage cart directly in the path of the arriving audience. The decision was made, in the teeth of powerful opposition, to extend the foyers towards the river, and to attempt to naturalise the exterior with plants and trees. It is entirely fitting that Eyre, passionate gardener, should be the person to green the National Theatre, just as he has throughout his period there diligently cultivated all of its working, nurturing, pruning where necessary, and above all planting seeds.

Another, festive, decision was taken, to play coloured lights on some of the building's larger surfaces. The installation during Peter Hall's régime of the running electric advertisement at the front of the building – again, vehemently opposed by the architect – had not only bruited forth the company's work, but had added a touch of celebration to the enterprise, much-needed, especially since Ralph's Rocket had ceased to streak across the skies over Waterloo Bridge. There is much to celebrate, after all. The record in terms of productions is without equal in the annals of the British theatre, and probably in the annals of any other theatre. The Company has been essentially pragmatic and eclectic, but it has pursued and maintained the highest standards in every department of the theatre's work. It has served as a public forum for the airing of themes of national concern, it has enabled and initiated the discovery of new means of theatrical expression, it has offered the best actors in the land rôles in an astonishingly wide range of work, it has commissioned new plays and adaptations from writers new and established, flourishing and forgotten. It has forged and sustained lively and cordial relations with the public, who have, over the years – give or take the odd stinker – supported its work loyally and enthusiastically. And it has done all this with minimal contributions from the governments of the day, and with tepid and ineffectual support from the Arts Council, during increasingly difficult times for the theatre in general. This success is due to the concerted efforts of the company at all levels and in every department, but it could not have happened without the tenacity of its artistic directors, three exceptional men who each gave up a large chunk of their lives, and large sums of money, to fight the good fight, because they believed in the idea enshrined in the National Theatre. Such people – men or women – are rare, and becoming rarer.

After much fevered discussion in the press and in green rooms everywhere, Richard Eyre's successor was named, to widespread relief, as Trevor Nunn, Peter Hall's successor at the RSC. One of the most successful directors of the age, gifted with political skill, talent, experience, influence and passion, he is the natural head of a great organisation. After some years as a freelance, he was motivated by a desire to plough back into the theatre what he had had out of it, and determined to ensure that the National Theatre and the theatre in general – for which this country has such special genius – remains central to the life of society, not a mere post-pre-show supper entertainment, or a pre-post-show dinner diversion, but – as John Osborne long ago defined it – a minority art with a majority influence, a crucible of ideas, the nation's story-board. The struggle to keep the theatre alive will never end; let us hope that we are training up a generation of tough fighters. The National Theatre will be the rallying point for the whole art, so its survival, and its glorious survival, is crucially important for all of us. "For a nation which loves its theatre," as Olivier wrote all those years ago, "is a healthy nation."

Ian Holm as King Lear, 1997
(Photo: John Haynes)

Richard Findlater was one of this country's most respected writers on the theatre. His drama criticism for a number of publications, and for the BBC, was admired inside and outside the profession. As well as biographies of such luminaries as Redgrave, Ashcroft, Olivier, Richardson, Lilian Baylis, and the clown Grimaldi, his eighteen books include a definitive history of stage censorship, *Banned*, and an account of contemporary British theatre, *The Unholy Trade*, which made his name. He edited the arts pages of the *Observer*, and was assistant editor of the paper, from 1963 until his sudden death in 1985.

The Winding Road to King's Reach
by Richard Findlater (1977)

The vision of a National Theatre had hovered hazily above the British stage for over a century. Continental examples showed that the vision could be turned into a reality: France has had a National Theatre since 1680; Denmark, Sweden and Austria have had theirs for some two hundred years. Yet the first record of a specific British project dates from no earlier than 1848, when a London publisher – Effingham Wilson – prompted by the purchase in 1847 of Shakespeare's birthplace for the nation – issued two pamphlets proposing "A House for Shakespeare", in public ownership, where the works of "the world's greatest moral teacher" would be constantly performed. Several eminent Victorians – including two of the century's most successful playwrights, Lord Lytton and Tom Taylor – later spoke up for the ideals of a National Theatre. The visit to Britain in 1879 of the Comédie Française was a spur to enthusiasts. Among them was Matthew Arnold, who in 1880 published an essay urging our need for a Comédie Anglaise and ending with an exhortation "The theatre is irresistible: organise the theatre!" that became a slogan among later campaigners (who sometimes overlooked the fact that Arnold had attributed it to Sarah Bernhardt, in her "most caressing tones"). Yet there was no sustained support for such an institution as long as the country's leading actors kept alive the classical repertoire (notably, Shakespeare) in London and the provinces.

About a century ago the accessibility of the classics and the survival of the acting tradition were threatened by the emergence of the entertainment industry, with its economic dependence on long runs in London and their provincial tours. The ideals of a National Theatre (not necessarily modelled on French lines) began to gain increasingly wide acceptance – not least by actors. Among these the most conspicuous advocate was Henry Irving, who – speaking before a Social Science Congress – eloquently championed the National cause in 1878 (though he did not share Arnold's vision). This was the year in which he inaugurated at the Lyceum a managerial regime that seemed, to the late Victorian era, to be a kind of National Theatre in itself. Its collapse in the 1890s under severe economic pressures perhaps helped to point the need for an endowed, exemplary theatre of an entirely different kind from the speculative show business of even the most talented and enlightened of star soloists in private management.

The substantial history of the National Theatre movement begins in the year of Irving's death, 1904, when the critic William Archer (pioneer translator of Ibsen) collaborated with the young actor-director-author Harley Granville Barker in producing a detailed scheme (with estimates) for the casting, budget and repertoire of a National Theatre. This was at first circulated privately, with

Geoffrey Whitworth, then secretary of the National Theatre Committee, receives from Bernard Shaw, on Shakespeare's birthday 1938, the deeds for the Cromwell Gardens site, together with a symbolic twig and piece of earth. Also in the picture are Sir William Davison and Sir Robert Vansittart

Top: Queen Elizabeth, now the Queen Mother, laying the first foundation stone in 1951 – on a site next to the Festival Hall. When the Theatre was later variously resited around the South Bank, she is reported to have suggested that the stone should be put on castors. It is now in the foyer of the Royal National Theatre

Below left: Kenneth Tynan and Richard Findlater pose dressed as undertakers beside the theatre-less foundation stone to mourn the apparent death of the National dream (Photo: Michael Boys)

Below right: Peggy Ashcroft in *Happy Days*, the first play to open to the public in the new National Theatre on the South Bank (Photo: Zoë Dominic)

the prefatory approval of six leading actors and dramatists: Henry Irving, Squire Bancroft, John Hare, James Barrie, Arthur Pinero and Henry Arthur Jones. Meredith, Hardy, Bridges and Galsworthy were among other eminences who later added their support. Shaw, a friend of both Archer and Granville Barker, was a pillar of strength to the National movement for most of his life. When *A National Theatre* was published in 1907, the campaign began in earnest: and the vision of Archer and Granville Barker, who saw the National not as a museum or a monument or an elitist luxury, but as "visibly and unmistakably a popular institution, making a large appeal to the whole community", has persisted in the design that made their dream come true seventy years later.

The National Theatre movement gained impetus in the Edwardian era by combining forces with two other campaigns: one linked with the revaluation of Elizabethan staging, pioneered by William Poel and supported by the London Shakespeare League (founded in 1902); and another crusade that had also started around 1904, with more traditional and less expensive objectives, originating (like Effingham Wilson's scheme in 1848) in the veneration of Shakespeare not only as a dramatist but as a kind of household deity, or moral sage. Its begetter Richard Badger, was an octogenarian brewer who had "acquired a Shakespearean taste" when at school for two years in Stratford-upon-Avon, and who wanted to make some recognition to Shakespeare for the debt that the world (and Mr Badger) owed to him, by building a statue in his memory. The army of memorialists attracted by Mr Badger's appeal were, in due course, persuaded by the National Theatre campaigners that the best way of remembering Shakespeare would be to build a theatre where his plays might be performed throughout the year (the Shakespeare Memorial Theatre in Stratford was then open for only a few weeks annually). In 1908 the two sets of crusaders merged to form the Shakespeare Memorial National Theatre committee. An appeal for funds was launched, with an initial £70,000 from Carl Meyer (through the good offices of Mrs Alfred Lyttelton). In 1909 the committee issued a handbook listing the following aims for a "Shakespeare National Theatre":

1. to keep the plays of Shakespeare in its repertory;
2. to revive whatever else is vital in English classical drama;
3. to prevent recent plays of great merit from falling into oblivion;
4. to produce new plays and to further the development of the modern drama;
5. to produce translations or representative works of foreign drama, ancient and modern;
6. to stimulate the art of acting through the varied opportunities it will offer to members of the company.

These targets were devoutly, if mistily, kept in view during the next fifty years.

Zealots in and outside the theatrical profession, fired by the wish to commemorate the coming 300th anniversary of Shakespeare's death in 1616, combined to spread the gospel and to raise the cash. The good works included a Shakespeare Ball, a Shakespeare Pageant, a Shakespeare Exhibition. And in 1913 a site was acquired for the National Theatre in Bloomsbury – the first of five in the next forty years.

The first world war blocked the progress of the National Theatre movement. With the disappearance of the stability maintained by leading actor-managers and the domination of the stage by speculative finance, the need for a National Theatre became increasingly evident – but so did the economic and organisational difficulties. Archer and Granville Barker had assumed in 1904 that state aid was out of the question; and it seemed no more probable in the 1920s, when theatrical costs were far higher than ever before. The Meyer gift accumulated interest; funds were raised in many ways; money continued to be given by individual believers. (Many donors' names were lost when air raids destroyed the records, but those that survive are engraved on a plaque in the National Theatre's foyer.) Dedicated activists like Mrs Lyttelton, Sir Israel Gollancz and Geoffrey Whitworth (of the British Drama League) talked on. In 1930 Granville Barker brought out a revised edition of his pioneering book, urging the need for two theatres under one roof. There were many articles, letters to the press, debates, demonstrations. The idea of the National, propagated ardently, won new adherents. Yet the reality remained remote between the wars. The only material advance was the acquisition in 1938 of another site – in Cromwell Gardens, opposite the Victoria and Albert Museum. It was, as many people soon realised, in the wrong area of London. It was also too small – as were nearly all the other sites later considered, in Leicester Square, Belgravia, Trafalgar Square, and other quarters. But it was to serve a purpose in the protracted manoeuvres that led to the eventual construction of the National Theatre.

The movement's history repeated itself. Within a year of buying a site, a world war broke out. The movement stopped. But the second war, unlike the first, had a decisive effect on the fortunes of the National Theatre campaign. By the time that peace was signed its aim appeared, for the first time, to have become practical politics. For this there were three reasons:

1. State aid for the arts was introduced in 1940 by the establishment of CEMA (the Council for the Encouragement of Music and the Arts), later transformed into the Arts Council. It was no longer, as it had seemed in 1904 to Archer and Granville Barker, "A waste of time" to look to Parliament for funds.

2. About 1942 the London County Council, considering the post-war development of the South Bank of the Thames, made approaches to the SMNT committee about the possible gift of a site there (anticipated in 1930 by Granville Barker) in exchange for the land in Cromwell Gardens.

3. Towards the end of the war, the Old Vic organisation put out feelers to the SMNT committee, with a view to association in creating the National Theatre.

In 1946 the wagon started to roll. The LCC presented a site between Waterloo Bridge and the site of the future Festival Hall. The Governors of the Old Vic and the Trustees of the Shakespeare Memorial Theatre made a "contract of betrothal" (as it was called by Oliver Lyttelton, later Lord Chandos) to get the National Theatre built – at which time the marriage of the two charities would be solemnised by Royal Charter. A Joint Council was appointed, with the prime task of selecting an architect. In 1948 the Chancellor of the Exchequer promised that the Treasury would – if the necessary legislation was passed – contribute up to a million pounds to the construction of a National Theatre, if the LCC provided the site. And in the following year, history was made, halfway, when the National Theatre Bill – enabling such a subsidy to be given, at the Chancellor's discretion – was passed without a division (on 21 January 1949). The figure of a million pounds made no allowance for the equipment of the theatre, nor for its annual running costs. The importance of the Bill was, indeed, symbolic, not practical. The principle had been established, but its implementation was to be postponed – indefinitely, it came to seem.

Another symbolic gesture was made two years later when a foundation stone was laid by Queen Elizabeth (now the Queen Mother) and dedicated by the Archbishop of Canterbury. Dame Sybil Thorndike read a poem, especially composed by the Poet Laureate, John Masefield. It was another historic non-event. A year later the site was quietly changed. The foundation stone was moved. It was the only thing that *did* move.

Nearly ten years passed before anything material happened. In spite of the National Theatre Act, in spite of the widespread support inside and outside the profession, it seemed all too possible that nothing would ever happen, that *no* Chancellor would judge the time ripe enough for investment in a National Theatre. Sceptics found confirmation in occasional stonewalling Ministerial speeches. A number of main factors rescued the project from paralysis in the 1960s. One was the imagination and zeal of a few people on both sides of the political fence in Parliament (notably, Jennie Lee and Oliver Lyttelton) and in the Arts Council (conspicuously Lord Cottesloe, then its chairman, and Lord Goodman, who succeeded him). Another crucial factor was the initiative of the LCC under Isaac Hayward's leadership: when in 1961 the Government declared that, in effect, the country could not afford a National Theatre, the LCC offered to pay half the cost of construction, in addition to providing the site rent free. Yet a third factor was that Hugh Jenkins, at the time a Labour Councillor, later Arts Minister, moved a resolution, carried unanimously – that the Theatre should be built without further delay. The Government then announced that it was ready to consider a National Theatre scheme, but only if the Stratford, Old Vic and Sadler's Wells organisations merged, and only if an opera house was built on the South Bank under the same roof. This proved to be impractical. Stratford withdrew from the attempted shotgun marriage in the following March. And in July 1962 the South Bank National Theatre and Opera House Board was set up to build the theatres on *two* sites given by the LCC between County Hall and Hungerford Bridge. It had also been decided to establish a National Theatre company without waiting for the building to be opened; and another body – the National Theatre Board – was established to run this company. The Trustees of the Old Vic granted the Board a lease of the old playhouse in the Waterloo Road. In August 1962 the first artistic director of the National Theatre company was named as Laurence Olivier. (He was then director of the Festival Theatre at Chichester, the first open stage playhouse to be built in Britain since Shakespeare's day.) They gave their first performance (*Hamlet*) at the Old Vic on 22 October 1963.

In the following month Denys Lasdun was appointed as architect (Lutyens and O'Rorke had submitted schemes on previous sites). Like his predecessors, he had never built a theatre. Unlike them he had made no preliminary plans and brought no preconceived ideas. For two years after his appointment he explored the problems with leading directors (Michael Benthall, Peter Brook, Michel St Denis, George Devine, John Dexter, Frank Dunlop, Michael Elliott, William Gaskill, and Peter Hall); four designers (Roger Furse, Jocelyn Herbert, Sean Kenny, Tanya Moiseiwitsch); a lighting designer (Richard Pilbrow); a manager (Stephen Arlen); and an actor (Robert Stephens). Kenneth Tynan, then literary manager of the National Theatre company, was also consulted.

In 1960 it had been planned to build both a proscenium stage and an arena theatre, each with some 1200 seats. Later the brief changed to one main, adaptable amphitheatre, combining an apron stage with a proscenium arch; and a second, small theatre seating about 400, "mainly for experimental purposes". During Lasdun's discussions the idea of an adaptable theatre was jettisoned. What was needed, the building committee decided, was an open stage and a proscenium stage, with a studio/workshop as well. In May 1965 the architect presented his preliminary plans and model, for both a theatre and an opera house. But in March 1966 the Government decided to sanction only the National Theatre for the time being. The following year the Opera House scheme was shelved, and Denys Lasdun's plans for the National Theatre were approved by the National Theatre Board. They had to be adapted to yet another site given by the GLC (successor to the LCC): the 4.7 acre Princes Meadow on King's Reach. Here work began on 3 November 1969, twenty years after the passing of the National Theatre Act, with shovels symbolically wielded by Jennie Lee; Lord Chandos, chairman of the National Theatre Board; Lord Cottesloe, chairman of the South Bank Board; and Desmond Plummer, then leader of the GLC. Four years later it was "topped out" by Laurence Olivier and Lord Cottesloe. In March 1973, after two serious bouts of illness, Olivier ended his ten highly successful years as director of the National Theatre company and was succeeded by Peter Hall.

The National Theatre was scheduled to open in April 1975; but there were severe and continuing building delays, because of the demands of specialist labour and the problems of getting innovatory equipment made to measure, installing it and testing it. Nothing like this had been built or designed before in Britain: it took far more time, patience and money than had been expected (with the help of Lord Eccles, then Minister with responsibility for the arts, the government limit of £3 75 million – half the estimated capital cost, the LCC undertaking the other half – had been raised in 1973 to £9.8 million, but by 1976 delays and inflation were to cause a further rise of some 70%).

Eventually it was decided to open the Theatre in phases, in order to avoid any further frustration and procrastination. On 16 March 1976 the Lyttelton (though not even then fully complete) opened its doors with productions transferred from the Old Vic, leading with Dame Peggy Ashcroft in Beckett's *Happy Days*. The Olivier (together with half the bars and buffets and, later, the restaurant) was launched in October 1976 with Albert Finney in the full text of Marlowe's *Tamburlaine The Great*, directed by Peter Hall. The Cottesloe staged its first public performances – a visit by the Science Fiction Theatre of Liverpool in Ken Campbell's and Chris Langham's epic show *Illuminatus!* – in March 1977.

Only when all three of the playhouses were in full swing, with the great organism of which they form a part, could the real history of the National Theatre be said to have begun.

EDITED EXTRACTS FROM A PLATFORM DISCUSSION BETWEEN
RICHARD EYRE & PETER HALL,
CHAIRED BY SUE MACGREGOR

This discussion took place in the Olivier Theatre on 25 October 1996, the 20th anniversary of the Royal opening of the National Theatre

SM On my left is Richard Eyre who succeeded Peter Hall to the Artistic Directorship in 1988. Peter Hall, on my right, was Director here for 15 years from 1973. Twenty years ago tonight, was the royal gala opening performance in this theatre. Do you remember that occasion very well, Peter?

PH Yes. That night was just a kind of formal blessing. For years we hadn't known whether the place would be open, whether it would be ready, what plays we could put on. Something about British builders, you know…

SM You did have a terribly difficult first few years here, indeed I think you and Denys Lasdun who designed this building, disagreed about how many theatres there should be in it. You wanted only two?

PH This goes back to the Building Committee. Peter Brook, Michel St Denis, George Devine and I did a minority report. We thought there should be one main auditorium and a studio, a laboratory. Olivier thought there had to be a proscenium theatre. "Where" he said "could I invite the Comédie Française if I didn't have a proscenium theatre?" and Kenneth Tynan, who was the National's dramaturg at the time, said if a proscenium arch was good enough for Brecht then it's good enough for us. And they prevailed, which was OK because they were the bosses at the time. I still think that it was a mistake because the problem is that there is no common aesthetic between the two larger theatres.

SM I'm sure you don't want to dwell on those early days too much, but you did have huge problems with the unions and so on.

PH Well more than that. We had problems with the fact that this country hates anything new, absolutely *loathes* it. The media and the profession loathed the very idea of the place, and did everything they could to stop it. The only people who liked it from day one were the public, and if that hadn't been so we wouldn't be here.

SM Jumping ahead to 1988 when you came here, Richard – by then it was the *Royal* National Theatre. Was that coincidental?

RE Actually I resisted it very strongly because I think it's an oxymoron – Royal National. I also thought that one of the glorious things about the National Theatre was precisely that it was one of the few great British institutions which *didn't* have the word Royal attached to it. This meant no disrespect and wasn't particularly a political point of view. I just thought it was making the National Theatre more like every other British organisation and I wanted it to be *extra*ordinary – a theatre for the nation. But sadly I lost out.

SM You took over a more than going concern, Richard, a hugely successful theatrical complex, but I imagine you wanted to make it feel a rather different place, however much you admired Peter's work, from the place he was running. How did you achieve that?

RE It was certainly much easier for me, coming into a going concern. I didn't have problems with the builders, I didn't have problems with the unions, and I didn't have problems with public opinion. From a real schism within the theatre, Peter did establish the National Theatre and make it appear a natural heart of the anatomy of theatre in this country. Of course I wanted it to be different, in the same way Trevor Nunn will. It must reflect his taste and his personality. I suppose I evolved what Peter might describe as an aesthetic (though I'd be slightly wary of using the word, because I think I'm more pragmatic than

Peter). I was made to concentrate my mind on what theatre is and become evangelical about the medium. I became interested in what I describe (as Robert Frost said of poetry) as the untranslatable element of theatre. I've become more and more interested in what is theatrical, what is the essence of a theatrical occasion.

SM I'm surprised to hear you say "the untranslatable", because one of the first really successful productions we all associate you with, from before you took over, is *Guys and Dolls*, which was hugely successful, and which you're putting on again.

RE Yes, well that's a very good example of what I mean by untranslatable: that it can't be translated into any other medium. You've got to be here in order to enjoy it.

PH I think *Guys and Dolls* is one of the best things the National has done and I was very proud and pleased that Richard did it in my time, but as far as some of the Board and most of the media were concerned before we did it, it was utterly absurd that the National should think it could do an American musical. There was a feeling at that time among the press and certain evangelical members of the profession, that the National Theatre existed in order to do verse drama about primitive Indians to an audience of three.

SM It's interesting that there has never been a National Theatre Company as such. Perhaps there was in the early days at the Old Vic under Sir Laurence Olivier. I remember then one could see Charles Kay, Ronald Pickup, Geraldine McEwan for example in successive productions. But since then not. Why is that?

RE I think it's partly that the climate is different, During the 80s all of us – and I hate it when people say "Mrs Thatcher did this"; actually all of us are responsible for what happened in the 80s, maybe because we were too supine to prevent it – we allowed a real change of climate, where opportunism became the prevailing virus. What happened also, was declining funding and declining confidence in regional theatre. When I was in regional theatre, there was a kind of ad hoc apprenticeship, so that actors like for instance Jonathan Pryce and Antony Sher, who

blossomed in my company at Nottingham, would consider it right that they should do three or four years around regional theatres before going into the movies or TV or coming to the National. People now feel they don't have the time. You could say that there's been a kind of cultural corrosion, similar to American showbiz culture.

SM Remind us of some of the productions you're most proud of, Peter.

PH I don't think I can, there's an enormous list and I don't live in the past. I was certainly proud of the fact, and it's something Richard has developed magnificently, and much better, that the most important plays in this complex have been new writing. That's been terrific and I don't think it's been sufficiently recognised. A new generation – David Hare, David Edgar, Howard Brenton – came to join the Pinters and Stoppards in my time.

SM What about Tony Harrison's *The Oresteia*?

PH *The Oresteia* was the sort of thing that only a place like this can do. We rehearsed and researched that for six months. I've just been back doing *The Oedipus Plays* at Richard's invitation, and again I had nearly four months in order to work out a different language of theatre. That's terribly valuable, that facility, and only a National Theatre can give you that.

SM Richard, did you know from the start that you had a winner on your hands with the Hare trilogy?

RE *Racing Demon* was originally going to be a sort of quasi-documentary, based on the Synod, which is actually shaped rather like the Olivier Theatre. If you go to the Synod there are about 1200 people, all vicars, and all incredibly rude to each other. They preface every insult with "It causes me great anguish to say this..." David fell in love with that world, and with the idea of decent people trying to do their best and to leave the world a better place than when they came into it. The idea of a trilogy of plays about people and institutions who exist in order to try and improve the world, I thought, was an absolutely irresistible project. It seemed a great folly – a *grand projet* in the French mode, like La

Défense arch – to say "We're going to do the three estates in the Olivier theatre and there will be a whole day that starts with the church in the morning, goes into the law in the afternoon, and politics in the evening". Nowhere else in the world could you do that. Like *The Oresteia*, which I thought was another grand folly, and magnificent.

PH   I think if you asked a computer what we ought to do in the theatre, it would evaluate what has happened in the past and what audiences have liked, and tell you what to do, and it would be a failure without question.

SM   There has been a criticism that the National Theatre has been insufficiently national. In other words that it hasn't toured enough. Is that valid?

PH   I don't think you could say that, particularly on Richard's record of the past few years. My vision when I first came here was that we should go out and play the large regional theatres and that they should come here. It happened twice. The Arts Council was craven, cowardly, didn't actually want to get behind it, thought it would give too much power to this building, so instead they encouraged division between the National and the regions and messed the whole thing up.

SM   Is that true, Richard?

RE   Yes, I think it probably is. Actually I'm feeling slightly shifty as Peter says that, because I was one of a number of regional theatre directors who signed a letter to *The Times*...

PH   I'm glad you brought that up...

RE   ...so I think you can date it by the notion of anyone thinking there would be the slightest atom achieved by writing a letter to *The Times*! We said we feared that all the resources of the theatre, our technicians, actors, directors, would be sucked into the centre. It actually turns out to have been a prophecy with some truth in it because what happened was that the National Theatre was built, the RSC expanded in some sense to mimic the National Theatre, and things *were* sucked to the centre. That's where I join you, Peter, in castigating the Arts Council.

PH   I don't believe it was because of the coming of the National Theatre that the regions suffered. The regions suffered because the Arts Council was progressively underfunded. Ask yourself how would the theatre be if the National Theatre hadn't happened? It would have much less writing talent, much less technical talent, much less acting talent, and most of all, much less audience for the future. The theatre is dying in America because there aren't any audiences being bred up. The RSC and the National are preserving the audience and renewing it for the future. That must be good.

Audience question
Would both gentlemen like to speculate about the developments they see in the next twenty years?

RE   I would say two of the most inspirational pieces of work that I've put on during my time would be *Angels in America*, Tony Kushner's play, and Robert Lepage's work. For both of them, subject matter and form were important, but the form followed the subject matter. I don't think we're going to see the theatre becoming technological. You can't computerise it. That's the joy of it and that's why it has to stay alive. The only thing I would say we're doing – and I wish I'd done it a long time ago – is making the Olivier temporarily into a theatre-in-the-round. Where we're sitting will be an oval shaped playing area. I think that will emancipate the space and be wonderful.

PH   My wishes for the future are more boring in a way. I'd like to see the government review the way it finances drama students because it's almost impossible for a young actor of talent to get trained unless he has existing resources. And I certainly would like to see a great deal of money poured into regional theatres, because the regions are where tomorrow's talent is born and audiences can be nurtured.

Audience question
Assuming Trevor Nunn invites you both back, what would be top of your list to direct? Will it be a new play, a classic?

RE   I think it would be most likely to be a new play. I'm rather bad at imagining what I would do.

Nancy Crane and Stephen
Dillane in *Angels in America*:
Perestroika, 1993
(Photo: John Haynes)

PH I think it would be a classic, because I suppose what I like most about being a director is that somebody pays me money to live inside Chekhov's head, or Ibsen's head, or Shakespeare's head, for a few weeks, to understand those masterpieces in a way that you can't by studying, you really can't. You find out where they are alive, and that's a great privilege, I enjoy that. I like doing that every day.

Audience question

What I am interested in is new audiences: how do you attract children and young people into the theatre?

PH In the last few years there has been less and less money to take children to live performances. Since 1979-1980 the subsidised theatre has been told you must charge what the market can bear. The idea of subsidy after the last war was that it would make available the arts to anybody who had a liking or a need for them. Why don't more kids come to the National Theatre? Because it's too expensive. If you could have popular prices there would be an even wider range of audience, I think.

Audience question:

With your experience as directors of the National Theatre, what would your advice to Trevor Nunn be?

PH Actually, I did give Trevor a piece of advice. It was fervent, passionate, and I meant it from the depths of my being. It was "Do it!" And I really couldn't say anything else.

RE My advice would be the same as Peter passed on to me, which was to remind me that the Olivier is the boiler house of the National Theatre: you neglect it at your peril. This is actually quite a profound piece of advice because it's not only describing the financial ecology of the National Theatre, but it's also saying remember, there is this magnificent auditorium that demands productions that speak to a large number of people. You have to find a way of reinventing theatre so that it works in here.

SM Trevor Nunn said the other day that he thought the West End might be the death of theatre in London. What is the state of the National Theatre that is being handed over to him now, after twenty years?

PH I think it's in terribly good nick. Richard has consolidated the force of public support, taken it into new areas – new writing, children's theatre. I think people love coming here because they can park, they can eat, they're not hassled or pushed around, there's music playing. It's a pleasant place to come, it's a serious place to come. If it wasn't here I do believe the theatre would be in quite a dangerous state. I think we got a National Theatre and a Royal Shakespeare Theatre just about in time. If we hadn't we'd be the same as Broadway – dead.

RE It would be vain of me to say the National is in good shape. I believe it *is* because I can check the audience statistics, which are a reasonable index but not the only one. The index is the spiritual health of it, and I've always believed that the remarkable thing about this organisation is that the whole is greater than the sum of its parts. You have a repertoire system that allows you to take risks, you have three theatres, Platform performances, music, an education department, a research and development department in the Studio, we tour all over the country and abroad, we have co-productions, we have visiting companies. This is a healthy organism, and it's a healthy organism because a lot of people were very brave and very dogged twenty years ago, and chief amongst those was Peter.

A CHRONOLOGICAL LIST OF ALL THE PLAYS PRESENTED BY THE NATIONAL THEATRE FROM 1963 TO 1997

The four hundred and eighty one plays listed here are those that the National has given on its main stages since its inception. Transfers, revivals, Sunday night performances, Platform performances, occasional workshops and Studio nights, Young Theatre Festivals, as well as seasons at the Young Vic, Jeanetta Cochrane, and ICA could not be recorded because of pressure on space, nor, for the same reason, could regional tours. The dates given are of a production's press night at the National.

Visiting productions are listed separately, at the end.

Jeanne Hepple, Mary Miller, Joan Plowright, Frank Finlay, and Michael Redgrave in *Hobson's Choice*, 1964 (Photo: Sandra Lousada)

1963

HAMLET
by William Shakespeare
Dir. Laurence Olivier
Old Vic 22 October

SAINT JOAN
by Bernard Shaw
Dir. John Dexter
Old Vic 30 October

UNCLE VANYA
by Anton Chekhov
trans. by Constance Garnett
Dir. Laurence Olivier
Old Vic 19 November

THE RECRUITING OFFICER
by George Farquhar
Dir. William Gaskill
Old Vic 10 December

1964

HOBSON'S CHOICE
by Harold Brighouse
Dir. John Dexter
Old Vic 7 January

ANDORRA
by Max Frisch
trans. by Michael Bullock
Dir. Lindsay Anderson
Old Vic 28 January

PLAY
by Samuel Beckett
Dir. George Devine
and
PHILOCTETES
by Sophocles,
adapted by Keith Johnstone
Dir. William Gaskill
Old Vic 7 April

OTHELLO
by William Shakespeare
Dir. John Dexter
Old Vic 23 April

THE MASTER BUILDER
by Henrik Ibsen
adapted by Emlyn Williams
Dir. Peter Wood
Old Vic 9 June

THE DUTCH COURTESAN
by John Marston
Dir. William Gaskill &
Piers Haggard
Old Vic 13 October

HAY FEVER
by Noël Coward
Dir. Noël Coward
Old Vic 27 October

THE ROYAL HUNT
OF THE SUN
by Peter Shaffer
Dir. John Dexter &
Desmond O'Donovan
Old Vic 8 December

1965

THE CRUCIBLE
by Arthur Miller
Dir. Laurence Olivier
Old Vic 19 January

MUCH ADO ABOUT
NOTHING
by William Shakespeare
with textual revisions by
Robert Graves
Dir. Franco Zeffirelli
Old Vic 16 February

MOTHER COURAGE AND
HER CHILDREN
by Bertolt Brecht
trans. by Eric Bentley,
lyrics trans. by W H Auden,
music by Paul Dessau
Dir. William Gaskill
Old Vic 12 May

ARMSTRONG'S LAST
GOODNIGHT
by John Arden
Devised by John Dexter &
William Gaskill
Proscenium production
Albert Finney
Old Vic 12 October

LOVE FOR LOVE
by William Congreve
Dir. Peter Wood
Old Vic 20 October

TRELAWNY OF THE WELLS
by Arthur W Pinero
Dir. Desmond O'Donovan
Old Vic 17 November

1966

A FLEA IN HER EAR
by Georges Feydeau
trans. by John Mortimer
Dir. Jacques Charon
Old Vic 8 February

MISS JULIE
by August Strindberg
trans. by Michael Meyer
Dir. Michael Elliott
and
BLACK COMEDY
by Peter Shaffer
Dir. John Dexter
Old Vic 8 March

JUNO AND THE PAYCOCK
by Sean O'Casey
Dir. Laurence Olivier
Old Vic 26 April

A BOND HONOURED
by John Osborne
(based on Lope de Vega)
Dir. John Dexter
(presented with *Black Comedy*,
as above)
Old Vic 6 June

THE STORM
by Alexander Ostrovsky
adapted by Doris Lessing
Dir. John Dexter
Old Vic 18 October

1967

THE DANCE OF DEATH
by August Strindberg
trans. by C D Locock
Dir. Glen Byam Shaw
Old Vic 21 February

ROSENCRANTZ AND
GUILDENSTERN ARE DEAD
by Tom Stoppard
Dir. Derek Goldby
Old Vic 11 April

THREE SISTERS
by Anton Chekhov
trans. by Moura Budberg
Dir. Laurence Olivier
Old Vic 4 July

AS YOU LIKE IT
by William Shakespeare
Dir. Clifford Williams
Old Vic 3 October

TARTUFFE
by Molière
trans. by Richard Wilbur
Dir. Tyrone Guthrie
Old Vic 21 November

Left: Joyce Redman and
Laurence Olivier in *Love for
Love*, 1965
(Photo: Zoë Dominic)

Right: Louise Purnell, Jeanne
Watts and Joan Plowright in
Three Sisters, 1967
(Photo: Zoë Dominic)

1968

VOLPONE
by Ben Jonson
Dir. Tyrone Guthrie
Old Vic 16 January

OEDIPUS
by Seneca
adapted by Ted Hughes from
trans. by David Anthony Turner
Dir. Peter Brook
Old Vic 19 March

EDWARD II
by Bertolt Brecht, after
Christopher Marlowe
trans. by William E Smith &
Ralph Manheim
Dir. Frank Dunlop
Old Vic 30 April

TRIPLE BILL
The Covent Garden Tragedy
by Henry Fielding
Dir. Robert Lang
A Most Unwarrantable Intrusion
by John Maddison Morton
Dir. Robert Stephens
In His Own Write
by John Lennon, Adrienne
Kennedy, Victor Spinetti
Dir. Victor Spinetti
Old Vic 18 June

THE ADVERTISEMENT
by Natalia Ginzburg
trans. by Henry Reed
Dir. Donald MacKechnie &
Laurence Olivier
Old Vic 24 September

HOME AND BEAUTY
by W Somerset Maugham
Dir. Frank Dunlop
Old Vic 8 October

LOVE'S LABOUR'S LOST
by William Shakespeare
Dir. Laurence Olivier
Old Vic 19 December

1969

'H' *or Monologues at Front of
Burning Cities*
by Charles Wood
Dir. Geoffrey Reeves
Old Vic 13 February

THE WAY OF THE WORLD
by William Congreve
Dir. Michael Langham
Old Vic 1 May

MACRUNE'S GUEVARA
by John Spurling
Dir. Frank Dunlop &
Robert Stephens
and
RITES
by Maureen Duffy
Dir. Joan Plowright
Old Vic 27 May

BACK TO METHUSELAH
by Bernard Shaw
Dir. Clifford Williams with
Donald MacKechnie
Old Vic, Part I: 31 July,
Part II: 1 August

THE NATIONAL HEALTH
by Peter Nichols
Dir. Michael Blakemore
Old Vic 16 October

THE WHITE DEVIL
by John Webster
Dir. Frank Dunlop
Old Vic 13 November

THE TRAVAILS OF
SANCHO PANZA
by James Saunders
Dir. Donald MacKechnie &
Joan Plowright
Old Vic 18 December

1970

THE BEAUX' STRATAGEM
by George Farquhar
Dir. William Gaskill
Old Vic 8 April

THE MERCHANT OF
VENICE
by William Shakespeare
Dir. Jonathan Miller
Old Vic 28 April

HEDDA GABLER
by Henrik Ibsen
trans. by Michael Meyer
Dir. Ingmar Bergman
Cambridge Theatre 29 June

THE IDIOT
by Simon Gray
adapted from Dostoevsky's novel
Dir. Anthony Quayle
Old Vic 15 July

CYRANO
by Edmond Rostand
adapted by Patrick Garland
Dir. Patrick Garland
Cambridge Theatre 27 October

MRS WARREN'S
PROFESSION
by Bernard Shaw
Dir. Ronald Eyre
Old Vic 30 December

Kenneth Mackintosh and
Ronald Pickup in *In His Own
Write*, part of *Triple Bill*, 1968
(Photo: Chris J Arthur)

1971

THE ARCHITECT AND THE
EMPEROR OF ASSYRIA
by Fernando Arrabal
trans. by Jean Benedetti
Dir. Victor García
Old Vic 3 February

THE CAPTAIN OF
KÖPENICK
by Carl Zuckmayer
adapted by John Mortimer
Dir. Frank Dunlop
Old Vic 9 March

A WOMAN KILLED
WITH KINDNESS
by Thomas Heywood
Dir. John Dexter
Old Vic 7 April

CORIOLANUS
by William Shakespeare
Dir. Manfred Wekwerth &
Joachim Tenschert
Old Vic 6 May

THE RULES OF THE GAME
by Luigi Pirandello
English version by David Hare &
Robert Rietty
Dir. Anthony Page
New Theatre 15 June

AMPHITRYON 38
by Jean Giraudoux, taken from
adaptations by S N Behrman &
Roger Gellert
Dir. Laurence Olivier
New Theatre 23 June

TYGER
by Adrian Mitchell
with music by Mike Westbrook
Dir. Michael Blakemore &
John Dexter
New Theatre 20 July

DANTON'S DEATH
by Georg Büchner
adapted by John Wells
Dir. Jonathan Miller
New Theatre 3 August

THE GOOD NATUR'D MAN
by Oliver Goldsmith
Dir. John Dexter
Old Vic 9 December

LONG DAY'S JOURNEY
INTO NIGHT
by Eugene O'Neill
Dir. Michael Blakemore
New Theatre 21 December

1972

JUMPERS
by Tom Stoppard
Dir. Peter Wood
Old Vic 2 February

RICHARD II
by William Shakespeare
Dir. David William
Old Vic 29 March

THE SCHOOL FOR
SCANDAL
by Richard Brinsley Sheridan
Dir. Jonathan Miller
Old Vic 11 May

THE FRONT PAGE
by Ben Hecht and Charles
MacArthur
Dir. Michael Blakemore
Old Vic 6 July

'TIS PITY SHE'S A WHORE
by John Ford
Dir. Roland Joffé
Old Vic 18 July (Mobile)

MACBETH
by William Shakespeare
Dir. Michael Blakemore
Old Vic 9 November

Anthony Hopkins and Jim Dale
in *The Architect and The
Emperor of Assyria*, 1971
(Photo: Michael Childers)

1973

TWELFTH NIGHT
by William Shakespeare
Dir. Peter James
Old Vic 4 January (Mobile)

THE MISANTHROPE
by Molière
English version by Tony Harrison
Dir. John Dexter
Old Vic 22 February

THE CHERRY ORCHARD
by Anton Chekhov
translated by Ronald Hingley
Dir. Michael Blakemore
Old Vic 24 May

EQUUS
by Peter Shaffer
Dir. John Dexter
Old Vic 26 July

THE BACCHAE
by Euripides
adapted by Wole Soyinka
Dir. Roland Joffé
Old Vic 2 August

SATURDAY SUNDAY
MONDAY
by Eduardo de Filippo
trans. by Keith Waterhouse &
Willis Hall
Dir. Franco Zeffirelli
Old Vic 31 October

THE PARTY
by Trevor Griffiths
Dir. John Dexter
Old Vic 20 December

1974

MEASURE FOR MEASURE
by William Shakespeare
Dir. Jonathan Miller
Old Vic 15 January (Mobile)

THE TEMPEST
by William Shakespeare
Dir. Peter Hall
Old Vic 5 March

EDEN END
by JB Priestley
Dir. Laurence Olivier
Old Vic 4 April

NEXT OF KIN
by John Hopkins
Dir. Harold Pinter
Old Vic 2 May

SPRING AWAKENING
by Frank Wedekind
trans. by Edward Bond
Dir. Bill Bryden
Old Vic 28 May

THE MARRIAGE OF FIGARO
by Beaumarchais
trans. by John Wells
Dir. Jonathan Miller
Old Vic 9 July

ROMEO AND JULIET
by William Shakespeare
Dir. Bill Bryden
Old Vic 28 August (Mobile)

THE FREEWAY
by Peter Nichols
Dir. Jonathan Miller
Old Vic 1 October

GRAND MANOEUVRES
by A E Ellis
Dir. Michael Blakemore
Old Vic 3 December

1975

JOHN GABRIEL BORKMAN ⋆
by Henrik Ibsen
trans. by Inga-Stina Ewbank &
Peter Hall
Dir. Peter Hall
Old Vic 28 January

HEARTBREAK HOUSE
by Bernard Shaw
Dir. John Schlesinger
Old Vic 25 February

HAPPY DAYS ⋆
by Samuel Beckett
Dir. Peter Hall
Old Vic 13 March

NO MAN'S LAND ⋆
by Harold Pinter
Dir. Peter Hall
Old Vic 23 April

ENGAGED
by W S Gilbert
Dir. Michael Blakemore
Old Vic 6 August

PHAEDRA BRITANNICA
by Tony Harrison
after Racine
Dir. John Dexter
Old Vic 9 September

THE PLAYBOY OF THE
WESTERN WORLD
by J M Synge
Dir. Bill Bryden
Old Vic 29 October

HAMLET ⋆
by William Shakespeare
Dir. Peter Hall
Old Vic 10 December

JUDGEMENT
by Barry Collins
Dir. Peter Hall
Old Vic 18 December

Diana Rigg, Alaknanda
Samarth, and David Yelland
in *Phaedra Britannica*
(Photo Anthony Crickmay)

95

1976

PLUNDER *
by Ben Travers
Dir. Michael Blakemore
Old Vic 14 January

WATCH IT COME DOWN *
by John Osborne
Dir. Bill Bryden
Old Vic 24 February

BLITHE SPIRIT
by Noël Coward
Dir. Harold Pinter
Lyttelton 24 June

WEAPONS OF HAPPINESS
by Howard Brenton
Dir. David Hare
Lyttelton 14 July

TAMBURLAINE THE GREAT
by Christopher Marlowe
Dir. Peter Hall
Olivier 4 October

IL CAMPIELLO
by Carlo Goldoni
English version by Susanna
Graham-Jones & Bill Bryden
Dir. Bill Bryden
Olivier 26 October

THE FORCE OF HABIT
by Thomas Bernhard
trans. by Neville & Stephen
Plaice
Dir. Elijah Moshinsky
Lyttelton 9 November

COUNTING THE WAYS
by Edward Albee
Dir. Bill Bryden
Olivier 6 December

* These six productions, and
later *The Playboy of the Western
World*, transferred from the Old
Vic to the Lyttelton in March
1976, opening the new theatre on
the South Bank

1977

TALES FROM THE VIENNA
WOODS
by Ödön von Horváth
trans. by Christopher Hampton
Dir. Maximilian Schell
Olivier 26 January

BEDROOM FARCE
by Alan Ayckbourn
Dir. Alan Ayckbourn & Peter Hall
Lyttelton 16 March

JULIUS CAESAR
by William Shakespeare
Dir. John Schlesinger
Olivier 22 March

STRAWBERRY FIELDS
by Stephen Poliakoff
Dir. Michael Apted
Cottesloe 5 April

THE PASSION
from York Mystery Plays
version by the Company and
Tony Harrison
Dir. Bill Bryden &
Sebastian Graham-Jones
Cottesloe 25 April

VOLPONE
by Ben Jonson
Dir. Peter Hall
Olivier 26 April

FOUR TO ONE
by Gawn Grainger
Dir. Sebastian Graham-Jones
Cottesloe 18 May

STATE OF REVOLUTION
by Robert Bolt
Dir. Christopher Morahan
Lyttelton 26 May

TO THOSE BORN LATER
poems and songs of
Bertolt Brecht
Devised by Michael Kustow &
John Willett
Dir. Michael Kustow
Cottesloe 1 June

OLD MOVIES
by Bill Bryden
Dir. Bill Bryden
Cottesloe 16 June

THE MADRAS HOUSE
by Harley Granville Barker
Dir. William Gaskill
Olivier 22 June

THE CAMILLA RINGBINDER
SHOW
by Trevor Ray & Richard
Mangan
Dir. Sebastian Graham-Jones
Cottesloe 1 July

BOW DOWN
by Tony Harrison (writer) and
Harrison Birtwistle (music)
Dir. Walter Donohue
Cottesloe 5 July

SIR IS WINNING
by Shane Connaughton
Dir. Christopher Morahan
Cottesloe 25 August

THE PLOUGH AND
THE STARS
by Sean O'Casey
Dir. Bill Bryden
Olivier 20 September

THE LADY FROM MAXIM'S
by Georges Feydeau
trans. by John Mortimer
Dir. Christopher Morahan
Lyttelton 18 October

1978

LAVENDER BLUE
by John Mackendrick
Dir. Sebastian Graham-Jones
Cottesloe 10 November

HALF-LIFE
by Julian Mitchell
Dir. Waris Hussein
Cottesloe 17 November

THE COUNTRY WIFE
by William Wycherley
Dir. Peter Hall with Stewart
Trotter
Olivier 29 November

SIR GAWAIN AND THE
GREEN KNIGHT
adapted by Peter Stevens from
Brian Stone's trans. of C14 poem
Dir. Michael Bogdanov
Lyttelton 8 December

THE HUNCHBACK OF
NOTRE DAME
adapted from Victor Hugo by
Ken Hill
Dir. Michael Bogdanov
Cottesloe 30 December

THE GUARDSMAN
by Ferenc Molnár
English version by Frank Marcus
Dir. Peter Wood
Lyttelton 3 January

ROBERT LOWELL,
AMERICAN POET
Devised by Ian Hamilton &
Michael Kustow
Dir. Michael Kustow
Cottesloe 20 January

THE CHERRY ORCHARD
by Anton Chekhov
trans. by Michael Frayn
Dir. Peter Hall
Olivier 14 February

LOVE LETTERS ON
BLUE PAPER
by Arnold Wesker
Dir. Arnold Wesker
Cottesloe 15 February

LARK RISE
by Keith Dewhurst from
Flora Thompson's book
Dir. Bill Bryden &
Sebastian Graham-Jones
Cottesloe 29 March

PLENTY
by David Hare
Dir. David Hare
Lyttelton 12 April

DON JUAN COMES BACK
FROM THE WAR
by Ödön von Horváth
trans. by Christopher Hampton
Dir. Stewart Trotter
Cottesloe 18 April

BRAND
by Henrik Ibsen
trans. by Geoffrey Hill
Dir. Christopher Morahan
Olivier 25 April

LOST WORLDS
by Wilson John Haire
Dir. Robert Kidd
Cottesloe 25 May

MACBETH
by William Shakespeare
Dir. Peter Hall with John
Russell Brown
Olivier 6 June

AMERICAN BUFFALO
by David Mamet
Dir. Bill Bryden
Cottesloe 28 June

THE WOMAN
by Edward Bond
Dir. Edward Bond
Olivier 10 August

THE PHILANDERER
by Bernard Shaw
Dir. Christopher Morahan
Lyttelton 7 September

THE DOUBLE DEALER
by William Congreve
Dir. Peter Wood
Olivier 27 September

THE WORLD TURNED
UPSIDE DOWN
by Keith Dewhurst from
Christopher Hill's book
Dir. Bill Bryden &
Sebastian Graham-Jones
Cottesloe 2 November

BETRAYAL
by Harold Pinter
Dir. Peter Hall
Lyttelton 15 November

HAS "WASHINGTON" LEGS?
by Charles Wood
Dir. Geoffrey Reeves
Cottesloe 29 November

STRIFE
by John Galsworthy
Dir. Christopher Morahan
Olivier 30 November

HEROD
by Paul Mills
Director Sebastian Graham-Jones
Cottesloe 11 December

Maria Aitken and
Joan Hickson in
Bedroom Farce, 1977
(Photo: Anthony Crickmay)

1979

A FAIR QUARREL
by Thomas Middleton & William
Rowley
Dir. William Gaskill
Olivier 8 February

THE LONG VOYAGE HOME
by Eugene O'Neill
Dir. Bill Bryden
Cottesloe 20 February

THE FRUITS OF
ENLIGHTENMENT
by Lev Tolstoy
trans. by Michael Frayn
Dir. Christopher Morahan
Olivier 8 March

FOR SERVICES RENDERED
by W Somerset Maugham
Dir. Michael Rudman
Lyttelton 1 May

CLOSE OF PLAY
by Simon Gray
Dir. Harold Pinter
Lyttelton 24 May

DISPATCHES
from Michael Herr's book
adapted for the stage by Bill
Bryden & the Company
Dir. Bill Bryden
Cottesloe 6 June

UNDISCOVERED COUNTRY
by Arthur Schnitzler
in a version by Tom Stoppard
Dir. Peter Wood
Olivier 20 June

AS YOU LIKE IT
by William Shakespeare
Dir. John Dexter
Olivier 1 August

WINGS
by Arthur Kopit
Dir. John Madden
Cottesloe 15 August

DEATH OF A SALESMAN
by Arthur Miller
Dir. Michael Rudman
Lyttelton 20 September

RICHARD III
by William Shakespeare
Dir. Christopher Morahan
Olivier 4 October

AMADEUS
by Peter Shaffer
Dir. Peter Hall
Olivier 2 November

CANDLEFORD
by Keith Dewhurst from
Flora Thompson's book
Dir. Bill Bryden & Sebastian
Graham-Jones
Cottesloe 14 November

WHEN WE ARE MARRIED
by J B Priestley
Dir. Robin Lefevre
Lyttelton 12 December

THE WILD DUCK
by Henrik Ibsen
trans. by Christopher Hampton
Dir. Christopher Morahan
Olivier 13 December

1980

HUGHIE
by Eugene O'Neill
Dir. Bill Bryden
Cottesloe 22 January

THEE AND ME
by Philip Martin
Dir. Michael Rudman
Lyttelton 26 February

THE ICEMAN COMETH
by Eugene O'Neill
Dir. Bill Bryden
Cottesloe 4 March

OTHELLO
by William Shakespeare
Dir. Peter Hall
Olivier 20 March

EARLY DAYS
by David Storey
Dir. Lindsay Anderson
Cottesloe 22 April

THE BROWNING VERSION
and HARLEQUINADE
by Terence Rattigan
Dir. Michael Rudman
Lyttelton 13 May

SISTERLY FEELINGS
by Alan Ayckbourn
Dir. Alan Ayckbourn &
Christopher Morahan
Olivier 3/4 June

THE ELEPHANT MAN
by Bernard Pomerance
Dir. Roland Rees
Lyttelton 15 July

THE LIFE OF GALILEO
by Bertolt Brecht
trans. by Howard Brenton
Dir. John Dexter
Olivier 13 August

Greg Hicks, Sara Kestelman
and Simon Callow in *As
You Like It*, 1979
(Photo: Zoë Dominic)

1981

LINE 'EM
by Nigel Williams
Dir. Christopher Morahan
Cottesloe 18 August

WATCH ON THE RHINE
by Lillian Hellman
Dir. Mike Ockrent
Lyttelton 16 September

THE NATIVITY
(as Part I of *The Passion*)
from medieval mystery plays
version by the Company &
Tony Harrison
Dir. Bill Bryden
Cottesloe 23 September

THE ROMANS IN BRITAIN
by Howard Brenton
Dir. Michael Bogdanov
Olivier 16 October

THE PROVOK'D WIFE
by John Vanbrugh
Dir. Peter Wood
Lyttelton 28 October

THE CRUCIBLE
by Arthur Miller
Dir. Bill Bryden
Cottesloe 30 October

THE CARETAKER
by Harold Pinter
Dir. Kenneth Ives
Lyttelton 11 November

HIAWATHA
by Longfellow
adapted by Michael Bogdanov
Dir. Michael Bogdanov
Olivier 10 December

MAN AND SUPERMAN
by Bernard Shaw
Dir. Christopher Morahan
Olivier 22 January

THE TICKET-OF-LEAVE
MAN
by Tom Taylor
Dir. Piers Haggard
Cottesloe 12 February

A MONTH IN THE
COUNTRY
by Ivan Turgenev
trans. by Isaiah Berlin
Dir. Peter Gill
Olivier 19 February

DON JUAN
by Molière
trans. by John Fowles
Dir. Peter Gill
Cottesloe 7 April

MEASURE FOR MEASURE
by William Shakespeare
Dir. Michael Rudman
Lyttelton 14 April

SERJEANT MUSGRAVE'S
DANCE
by John Arden
Dir. John Burgess
Cottesloe 27 May

THE SHOEMAKERS'
HOLIDAY
by Thomas Dekker
Dir. John Dexter
Olivier 19 June

ONE WOMAN PLAYS
by Dario Fo & Franca Rame
version by Olwen Wymark
Dir. Michael Bogdanov
Cottesloe 26 June

TRANSLATIONS
by Brian Friel
Dir. Donald McWhinnie
Lyttelton 6 August
(transfer from Hampstead
Theatre)

THE MAYOR OF ZALAMEA
by Calderón
trans. by Adrian Mitchell
Dir. Michael Bogdanov
Cottesloe 12 August

MUCH ADO ABOUT
NOTHING
by William Shakespeare
Dir. Peter Gill
Olivier 14 August

WHO'S AFRAID OF VIRGINIA
WOOLF?
by Edward Albee
Dir. Nancy Meckler
Lyttelton 27 August

ON THE RAZZLE
by Tom Stoppard
adapted from Johann Nestroy
Dir. Peter Wood
Lyttelton 22 September

CARITAS
by Arnold Wesker
Dir. John Madden
Cottesloe 7 October

THE HYPOCHONDRIAC
by Molière
trans. by Alan Drury
Dir. Michael Bogdanov
Olivier 22 October

THE ORESTEIA
the trilogy by Aeschylus
in a version by Tony Harrison
Dir. Peter Hall
music by Harrison Birtwistle
Olivier 28 November

TRUE WEST
by Sam Shepard
Dir. John Schlesinger
Cottesloe 10 December

THE SECOND MRS
TANQUERAY
by Arthur W Pinero
Dir. Michael Rudman
Lyttelton 15 December

Gina Bellman, Caroline
Embling, Tracy Taylor,
and Colette Barker in
The Crucible, 1980
(Photo: Michael Mayhew)

1982

SUMMER
by Edward Bond
Dir. Edward Bond
Cottesloe 27 January

GUYS AND DOLLS
based on a story and characters
of Damon Runyon
music & lyrics by Frank Loesser
book by Jo Swerling & Abe
Burrows
Dir. Richard Eyre
choreography by David Toguri
MD Tony Britten
Olivier 9 March

THE PRINCE OF HOMBURG
by Heinrich von Kleist
in a version by John James
Dir. John Burgess
Cottesloe 22 April

UNCLE VANYA
by Anton Chekhov
in a version by Pam Gems
Dir. Michael Bogdanov
Lyttelton 18 May

DON QUIXOTE
a play by Keith Dewhurst from
the novel by Miguel de Cervantes
Dir. Bill Bryden
Olivier 18 June

THE BEGGAR'S OPERA
by John Gay
Dir. Richard Eyre
Cottesloe 1 July

DANTON'S DEATH
by Georg Büchner
in a version by Howard Brenton
Dir. Peter Gill
Olivier 21 July

THE CAUCASIAN
CHALK CIRCLE
by Bertolt Brecht
trans. by James & Tania Stern
with W H Auden
Dir. Michael Bogdanov &
Justin Greene
Cottesloe 2 August (Mobile)

THE IMPORTANCE OF
BEING EARNEST
by Oscar Wilde
Dir. Peter Hall
Lyttelton 16 September

THE SPANISH TRAGEDY
by Thomas Kyd
Dir. Michael Bogdanov
Cottesloe 22 September

SCHWEYK IN THE SECOND
WORLD WAR
by Bertolt Brecht
trans. by Susan Davies
music by Hanns Eisler
Dir: Richard Eyre
Olivier 23 September

WAY UPSTREAM
by Alan Ayckbourn
Dir. Alan Ayckbourn
Lyttelton 4 October

OTHER PLACES
Family Voices, Victoria Station,
A Kind of Alaska
by Harold Pinter
Dir. Peter Hall
Cottesloe 14 October

MAJOR BARBARA
by Bernard Shaw
Dir. Peter Gill
Lyttelton 27 October

A MIDSUMMER NIGHT'S
DREAM
by William Shakespeare
Dir. Bill Bryden
Cottesloe 25 November

1983

A MAP OF THE WORLD
by David Hare
Dir. David Hare
Lyttelton 27 January

KICK FOR TOUCH
by Peter Gill
Dir. Peter Gill
Cottesloe 15 February

SMALL CHANGE
by Peter Gill
Dir. Peter Gill
Cottesloe 23 February

LORENZACCIO
by Alfred de Musset
trans. & adapted by John Fowles
Dir. Michael Bogdanov
Olivier 15 March

THE RIVALS
by Richard Brinsley Sheridan
Dir. Peter Wood
Olivier 12 April

THE TROJAN WAR WILL
NOT TAKE PLACE
by Jean Giraudoux
English version by
Christopher Fry
Dir. Harold Pinter
Lyttelton 10 May

MACBETH
by William Shakespeare
Dir. Michael Bogdanov with
Justin Greene & Alan Cohen
Cottesloe 16 May (Mobile)

INNER VOICES
by Eduardo de Filippo
trans. by N F Simpson
Dir. Mike Ockrent
Lyttelton 16 June

THE FAWN
by John Marston
Dir. Giles Block
Cottesloe 14 July

YOU CAN'T TAKE IT
WITH YOU
by George S Kaufman &
Moss Hart
Dir. Michael Bogdanov
Lyttelton 4 August

1984

TALES FROM HOLLYWOOD
by Christopher Hampton
Dir. Peter Gill
Olivier 1 September

GLENGARRY GLEN ROSS
by David Mamet
Dir. Bill Bryden
Cottesloe 21 September

JEAN SEBERG
composer Marvin Hamlisch
lyricist Christopher Adler
dramatist Julian Barry
Dir. Peter Hall
Olivier 1 December

CINDERELLA
adapted by Bill Bryden, Trevor
Ray & the Company
Dir. Bill Bryden
Lyttelton 15 December

STRIDER – THE STORY
OF A HORSE
by Mark Rozovsky from a story
by Tolstoy
in a version by Peter Tegel
Dir. Michael Bogdanov
Cottesloe 26 January

SAINT JOAN
by Bernard Shaw
Dir. Ronald Eyre
Olivier 16 February

VENICE PRESERV'D
by Thomas Otway
Dir. Peter Gill
Lyttelton 12 April

ANIMAL FARM
by George Orwell
stage adaptation by Peter Hall
Lyrics by Adrian Mitchell,
Music by Richard Peaslee
Dir. Peter Hall
Cottesloe 25 April

ANTIGONE
by Sophocles
trans. by C A Trypanis
Dir. John Burgess & Peter Gill
Cottesloe 17 May

GOLDEN BOY
by Clifford Odets
Dir. Bill Bryden
Lyttelton 22 May

MANDRAGOLA
by Niccolo Machiavelli
trans. by Wallace Shawn
Dir. David Gilmore
Olivier 14 June

ANTON CHEKHOV
devised by Michael Pennington
Dir. Michael Pennington
Cottesloe 5 July

WILD HONEY
by Anton Chekhov
in a version by Michael Frayn
Dir. Christopher Morahan
Lyttelton 19 July

A LITTLE HOTEL
ON THE SIDE
by Georges Feydeau &
Maurice Desvallières
trans. by John Mortimer
Dir. Jonathan Lynn
Olivier 9 August

FOOL FOR LOVE
by Sam Shepard
Dir. Peter Gill
Cottesloe 4 October

ROUGH CROSSING
by Tom Stoppard
freely adapted from Molnár's
Play at the Castle
Dir. Peter Wood
Lyttelton 30 October

SHE STOOPS TO CONQUER
by Oliver Goldsmith
Dir. Giles Block
Lyttelton 8 November

THE ANCIENT MARINER
Samuel Taylor Coleridge's poem
adapted by Michael Bogdanov
Dir. Michael Bogdanov
Olivier 14 November

CORIOLANUS
by William Shakespeare
Dir Peter Hall
Olivier 15 December

Jack Shepherd and
Tony Haygarth in
Glengarry Glen Ross, 1983
(Photo: Nobby Clark)

1985

DOOMSDAY
presented with *The Nativity* and
The Passion
under the title of
THE MYSTERIES
from medieval mystery plays
version by the Company with
Tony Harrison
Dir. Bill Bryden
Cottesloe 19 January

THE GOVERNMENT
INSPECTOR
by Nikolai Gogol
in a new version by Adrian
Mitchell
Dir. Richard Eyre
Olivier 31 January

THE ROAD TO MECCA
by Athol Fugard
Dir. Athol Fugard
Lyttelton 27 February

MARTINE
by Jean-Jacques Bernard
trans. by John Fowles
Dir. Peter Hall
Lyttelton 20 April

PRAVDA
by Howard Brenton &
David Hare
Dir. David Hare
Olivier 2 May

THE DUCHESS OF MALFI
by John Webster
Dir. Philip Prowse
Lyttelton 4 July

A CHORUS OF
DISAPPROVAL
by Alan Ayckbourn
Dir. Alan Ayckbourn
Olivier 1 August 1985

THE REAL INSPECTOR
HOUND
by Tom Stoppard
Dir. Tom Stoppard
and
THE CRITIC
by Richard Brinsley Sheridan
Dir. Sheila Hancock
Olivier 12 September

FESTIVAL OF NEW PLAYS
THE MURDERERS
by Daniel Mornin
Dir. Peter Gill
Cottesloe 23 September
TRUE DARE KISS
by Debbie Horsfield
Dir. John Burgess
Cottesloe 3 October
AS I LAY DYING
by Peter Gill from
William Faulkner
Dir. Peter Gill
Cottesloe 15 October
COMMAND OR PROMISE
by Debbie Horsfield
Dir. John Burgess
Cottesloe 24 October
FIVE PLAY BILL:
A Twist of Lemon by Alex Renton
Dir. Peter Gill
Sunday Morning by Rod Smith
Dir. John Burgess
In the Blue by Peter Gill
Dir. Peter Gill
Bouncing by Rosemary Wilton
Dir. Peter Gill
Up for None by Mick Mahoney
Dir. Peter Gill
Cottesloe 6 November
THE GARDEN OF ENGLAND
edited by Peter Cox &
the Company
Dir. John Burgess & Peter Gill
Cottesloe 14 November

MRS WARREN'S
PROFESSION
by Bernard Shaw
Dir. Anthony Page
Lyttelton 10 October

LOVE FOR LOVE
by William Congreve
Dir. Peter Wood
Lyttelton 13 November

YONADAB
by Peter Shaffer
Dir. Peter Hall
Olivier 4 December

THE CHERRY ORCHARD
by Anton Chekhov
trans. by Mike Alfreds with Lilia
Sokolov
Dir. Mike Alfreds
Cottesloe 10 December

Rik Mayall in *The Government Inspector*, 1985 (Photo: John Haynes)

1986

HAMLET
by William Shakespeare
Dir. Cicely Berry
Cottesloe 9 January (Mobile)

NOT ABOUT HEROES
by Stephen MacDonald
Dir. Michael Simpson
Cottesloe 13 February

BRIGHTON BEACH
MEMOIRS
by Neil Simon
Dir. Michael Rudman
Lyttelton 25 February

THE THREEPENNY OPERA
by Bertolt Brecht & Kurt Weill
trans. by Robert David
MacDonald
Dir. Peter Wood
Olivier 13 March

FUTURISTS
by Dusty Hughes
Dir. Richard Eyre
Cottesloe 17 March

ONLY FOURTEEN LINES
a selection of Shakespeare's
sonnets
Devised by Frances de la Tour
and David Leveaux
Cottesloe 25 April

DOWN CEMETERY ROAD
the landscape of Philip Larkin
devised by Patrick Garland
Cottesloe 1 May

DALLIANCE
Arthur Schnitzler's *Liebelei*
in a version by Tom Stoppard
Dir. Peter Wood
Lyttelton 27 May

NEAPTIDE
by Sarah Daniels
Dir. John Burgess
Cottesloe 2 July

JACOBOWSKY AND THE
COLONEL
original play by Franz Werfel
English-language version by
S N Behrman
Dir. Jonathan Lynn
Olivier 22 July

THE PETITION
by Brian Clark
Dir. Peter Hall
Lyttelton 30 July

THE AMERICAN CLOCK
by Arthur Miller
Dir. Peter Wood
Cottesloe 6 August

THE BAY AT NICE
and
WRECKED EGGS
by David Hare
Dir. David Hare
Cottesloe 9 September

THE MAGISTRATE
by Arthur W Pinero
Dir. Michael Rudman
Lyttelton 24 September

TONS OF MONEY
by Will Evans & Valentine
Dir. Alan Ayckbourn
Lyttelton 6 November

THE PIED PIPER
by Adrian Mitchell
from Robert Browning
Devised & Dir. by Alan Cohen
Music Dominic Muldowney
Olivier 18 November

KING LEAR
by William Shakespeare
Dir. David Hare
Olivier 11 December

THE MOTHER
by Bertolt Brecht
trans. by Steve Gooch
Dir. Di Trevis
Cottesloe 11 December (Mobile)

1987

COMING IN TO LAND
by Stephen Poliakoff
Dir. Peter Hall
Lyttelton 7 January

THREE MEN ON A HORSE
by George Abbott &
John Cecil Holm
Dir. Jonathan Lynn
Cottesloe 22 January

SCHOOL FOR WIVES
by Molière
trans. by Robert David
MacDonald
Dir. Di Trevis
Lyttelton 29 January

A VIEW FROM THE BRIDGE
by Arthur Miller
Dir. Alan Ayckbourn
Cottesloe 12 February

SIX CHARACTERS IN
SEARCH OF AN AUTHOR
by Luigi Pirandello
version by Nicholas Wright
Dir. Michael Rudman
Olivier 18 March

YERMA
by Federico García Lorca
trans. by Peter Luke
Dir. Di Trevis
Cottesloe 26 March

ANTONY AND CLEOPATRA
by William Shakespeare
Dir. Peter Hall
Olivier 9 April

ROSMERSHOLM
by Henrik Ibsen
version by Frank McGuinness
Dir. Sarah Pia Anderson
Cottesloe 6 May

A SMALL FAMILY BUSINESS
by Alan Ayckbourn
Dir. Alan Ayckbourn
Olivier 21 May

FATHERS AND SONS
by Brian Friel, after Turgenev's
novel
Dir. Michael Rudman
Lyttelton 9 July

1988

MEAN TEARS
by Peter Gill
Dir. Peter Gill
Cottesloe 22 July

THE WANDERING JEW
by Micheline Wandor &
Mike Alfreds
from Eugène Sue's novel
Dir. Mike Alfreds
Lyttelton 8 August

TING TANG MINE
by Nick Darke
Dir. Michael Rudman
Cottesloe 23 September

ENTERTAINING
STRANGERS
by David Edgar
Dir. Peter Hall
Cottesloe 15 October

WAITING FOR GODOT
by Samuel Beckett
Dir. Michael Rudman
Lyttelton 25 November

COUNTRYMANIA
a trilogy by Carlo Goldoni
(*Country Fever, Country Hazards,
Country Harvest*)
in a version by Mike Alfreds
Dir. Mike Alfreds
Olivier 12 December

George Harris and
Miranda Richardson in
The Changeling, 1988
(Photo: John Haynes)

CAT ON A HOT TIN ROOF
by Tennessee Williams
Dir. Howard Davies
Lyttelton 3 February

A PLACE WITH THE PIGS
by Athol Fugard
Dir. Athol Fugard
Cottesloe 16 February

'TIS PITY SHE'S A WHORE
by John Ford
Dir. Alan Ayckbourn
Olivier 3 March

FANSHEN
by David Hare
Dir. Les Waters
Cottesloe 31 March (Mobile)

THE SHAUGHRAUN
by Dion Boucicault
Dir. Howard Davies
Olivier 11 May

THE WINTER'S TALE
by William Shakespeare
Dir. Peter Hall
Cottesloe 18 May

THE TEMPEST
by William Shakespeare
Dir. Peter Hall
Cottesloe 19 May

CYMBELINE
by William Shakespeare
Dir. Peter Hall
Cottesloe 20 May

THE STRANGENESS OF
OTHERS
by Nick Ward
Dir. Nick Ward
Cottesloe 21 June

THE CHANGELING
by Thomas Middleton &
William Rowley
Dir. Richard Eyre
Lyttelton 23 June

MRS KLEIN
by Nicholas Wright
Dir. Peter Gill
Cottesloe 10 August

WHEN WE WERE WOMEN
by Sharman Macdonald
Dir. John Burgess
Cottesloe 15 September (Studio)

THE SECRET RAPTURE
by David Hare
Dir. Howard Davies
Lyttelton 4 October

ROOTS
by Arnold Wesker
Dir: Simon Curtis
Cottesloe 19 October (Mobile)

BARTHOLOMEW FAIR
by Ben Jonson
Dir. Richard Eyre
Olivier 20 October

MOUNTAIN LANGUAGE
by Harold Pinter
Dir. Harold Pinter
Lyttelton 20 October

THE FATHER
by August Strindberg
in a new version by John Osborne
Dir. David Leveaux
Cottesloe 26 October

SINGLE SPIES
by Alan Bennett
An Englishman Abroad
Dir. Alan Bennett
and
A Question of Attribution
Dir. Simon Callow
Lyttelton 1 December

THE MAGIC OLYMPICAL
GAMES
by Graeme Garden
Dir. Ken Campbell
Olivier 8 December

1989

FUENTE OVEJUNA
by Lope de Vega, in a new
version by Adrian Mitchell
Dir: Declan Donnellan
Cottesloe 10 January

SPEED-THE-PLOW
by David Mamet
Dir. Gregory Mosher
Lyttelton 25 January

HEDDA GABLER
by Henrik Ibsen
in a new version by
Christopher Hampton
Dir. Howard Davies
Olivier 2 February

JUNO AND THE PAYCOCK
by Sean O'Casey
Dir. Peter Gill
Lyttelton 22 February

BED
by Jim Cartwright
Dir. Julia Bardsley
Cottesloe 8 March

HAMLET
by William Shakespeare
Dir. Richard Eyre
Olivier 16 March

MARCH ON RUSSIA
by David Storey
Dir. Lindsay Anderson
Lyttelton 6 April

GHETTO
by Joshua Sobol
in a version by David Lan
songs translated & music
arranged by Jeremy Sams
Dir. Nicholas Hytner
Olivier 27 April

THE MISANTHROPE
by Molière
English version by Tony Harrison
Dir. Paul Unwin
Lyttelton 31 May
(co-production with Bristol
Old Vic)

THE VOYSEY INHERITANCE
by Harley Granville Barker
Dir. Richard Eyre
Cottesloe 27 June

THE LONG WAY ROUND
by Peter Handke
trans. by Ralph Manheim
Dir. Stephen Unwin
Cottesloe 6 July (Studio)

SCHISM IN ENGLAND
by Calderon
in a new trans by John Clifford
Dir. John Burgess
Cottesloe 26 July (Studio)

MAN, BEAST AND VIRTUE
by Luigi Pirandello
in a new version by Charles Wood
Dir. William Gaskill
Cottesloe 7 September

THE MAGIC CARPET
devised by the Company
Dir. Stephen Unwin
Cottesloe 25 September

MA RAINEY'S BLACK
BOTTOM
by August Wilson
Dir. Howard Davies
Cottesloe 25 October

SALOME
by Oscar Wilde
Dir. Steven Berkoff
Lyttelton 7 November

THE BEAUX' STRATAGEM
by George Farquhar
Dir. Peter Wood
Lyttelton 14 November
(co-production with Belgrade,
Coventry)

THE GOOD PERSON OF
SICHUAN
by Bertolt Brecht
trans. by Michael Hofmann
Dir. Deborah Warner
Olivier 28 November

WHALE
by David Holman
Dir. Tim Supple
Lyttelton 12 December

1990

BENT
by Martin Sherman
Dir. Sean Mathias
Lyttelton 19 January

RACING DEMON
by David Hare
Dir. Richard Eyre
Cottesloe 8 February

PEER GYNT
by Henrik Ibsen
in an English version by
Kenneth McLeish
Dir. Declan Donnellan
Olivier 28 February

SUNDAY IN THE PARK
WITH GEORGE
Music & lyrics by
Stephen Sondheim
Book by James Lapine
Dir. Steven Pimlott
Lyttelton 15 March

THE TRACKERS OF
OXYRHYNCHUS
by Tony Harrison
Dir. Tony Harrison
Olivier 27 March

TARTUFFE
trans. from the play by Molière
Dir. Jatinder Verma
Cottesloe 19 April

THE SCHOOL FOR
SCANDAL
by Richard Brinsley Sheridan
Dir. Peter Wood
Olivier 24 April

BERENICE
by Jean Racine
trans. by Neil Bartlett
Dir. Tim Albery
Cottesloe 9 May

THE CRUCIBLE
by Arthur Miller
Dir. Howard Davies
Olivier 31 May

AFTER THE FALL
by Arthur Miller
Dir. Michael Blakemore
Cottesloe 20 June

RICHARD III
by William Shakespeare
Dir. Richard Eyre
Lyttelton 25 July

KING LEAR
by William Shakespeare
Dir. Deborah Warner
Lyttelton 26 July

PIANO
by Trevor Griffiths
Dir. Howard Davies
Cottesloe 8 August

ONCE IN A WHILE THE
ODD THING HAPPENS
by Paul Godfrey
Dir. Paul Godfrey
Cottesloe 18 September

MORE TALES FROM THE
MAGIC CARPET
stories from around the world
Devised by Chris Barton & the
Company
Dir. Chris Barton
Cottesloe 1 October

THE SHAPE OF THE TABLE
by David Edgar
Dir. Jenny Killick
Cottesloe 8 November

THE WIND IN THE
WILLOWS
by Kenneth Grahame
adapted by Alan Bennett
Dir. Nicholas Hytner
Olivier 12 December

1991

ACCIDENTAL DEATH OF AN
ANARCHIST
by Dario Fo
English version by Alan
Cumming & Tim Supple
Dir. Tim Supple
Cottesloe 4 January (Mobile)

THE FEVER
written & performed by
Wallace Shawn
Cottesloe 8 February
(co-production with Royal Court)

WHITE CHAMELEON
by Christopher Hampton
Dir. Richard Eyre
Cottesloe 14 February

THE TRIAL
by Franz Kafka
adapted by Steven Berkoff
Dir. Steven Berkoff
Lyttelton 5 March

INVISIBLE FRIENDS
by Alan Ayckbourn
Dir. Alan Ayckbourn
Cottesloe 13 March

BLACK SNOW
by Keith Dewhurst
from the novel by
Mikhail Bulgakov
Dir. William Gaskill
Cottesloe 25 April

THE MISER
by Molière
in a new trans. by
Jeremy Sams
Dir. Steven Pimlott
Olivier 9 May

LONG DAY'S JOURNEY
INTO NIGHT
by Eugene O'Neill
Dir. Howard Davies
Lyttelton 21 May
(co-production with Bristol
Old Vic)

THE WHITE DEVIL
by John Webster
Dir. Philip Prowse
Olivier 13 June

NAPOLI MILIONARIA
by Eduardo de Filippo
English version by
Peter Tinniswood
Dir. Richard Eyre
Lyttelton 27 June

Diana Kent and Kenneth
Cranham in *An Inspector
Calls*, 1992
(Photo: Ivan Kyncl)

1992

THE COUP
by Mustapha Matura
Dir. Roger Michell
Cottesloe 18 July

THE RESISTIBLE RISE
OF ARTURO UI
by Bertolt Brecht
trans. by Ranjit Bolt
Dir. Di Trevis
Olivier 8 August

AT OUR TABLE
by Daniel Mornin
Dir. Jenny Killick
Cottesloe 19 September

MURMURING JUDGES
by David Hare
Dir. Richard Eyre
Olivier 10 October

THE MADNESS OF
GEORGE III
by Alan Bennett
Dir. Nicholas Hytner
Lyttelton 28 November

THE LITTLE CLAY CART
attributed to Shudraka
new version by Jatinder Verma
additional verse & songs by
Ranjit Bolt
Dir. Jatinder Verma
Cottesloe 5 December

THE SEA
by Edward Bond
Dir. Sam Mendes
Lyttelton 12 December

BLOOD WEDDING
by Federico García Lorca
trans. by Gwenda Pandolfi
Dir. Yvonne Brewster
Cottesloe 17 December (Mobile)

ANGELS IN AMERICA
Part One: *Millennium Approaches*
by Tony Kushner
Dir. Declan Donnellan
Cottesloe 23 January

THE NIGHT OF THE
IGUANA
by Tennessee Williams
Dir. Richard Eyre
Lyttelton 6 February

UNCLE VANYA
by Anton Chekhov
version by Pam Gems
Dir. Sean Mathias
Cottesloe 25 February (Studio)

THE RECRUITING OFFICER
by George Farquhar
Dir. Nicholas Hytner
Olivier 12 March

PYGMALION
by Bernard Shaw
Dir. Howard Davies
Olivier 9 April

LE BOURGEOIS
GENTILHOMME
by Molière, with music by
Jean-Baptiste Lully
version by Nick Dear
Dir. Richard Jones
Lyttelton 5 May

THE RISE AND FALL OF
LITTLE VOICE
by Jim Cartwright
Dir. Sam Mendes
Cottesloe 16 June 1992

A MIDSUMMER NIGHT'S
DREAM
by William Shakespeare
Dir. Robert Lepage
Olivier 9 July

STREET OF CROCODILES
based on stories by Bruno Schulz
devised by the Company from an
adaptation by Simon McBurney
& Mark Wheatley
Dir. Simon McBurney
Cottesloe 13 August
(co-production with Theatre
de Complicite)

AN INSPECTOR CALLS
by J B Priestley
Dir: Stephen Daldry
Lyttelton 11 September

KINGS
an account of Books I & II of
Homer's *Iliad*
by Christopher Logue
Dir. Liane Aukin
Cottesloe 17 September

SQUARE ROUNDS
by Tony Harrison
Dir: Tony Harrison
Olivier 1 October

DRAGON
by Yevgeny Shvarts
Eng. version by
Alan Cumming & Ultz
Dir. Ultz
Olivier 6 November

STAGES
by David Storey
Dir. Lindsay Anderson
Cottesloe 18 November

CAROUSEL
music by Richard Rodgers
book & lyrics by Oscar
Hammerstein
based on the play *Liliom* by
Ferenc Molnar
as adapted by Benjamin F Glaser
Dir. Nicholas Hytner
Choreography Kenneth
MacMillan
Lyttelton 10 December

BILLY LIAR
by Keith Waterhouse &
Willis Hall
Dir. Tim Supple
Cottesloe 15 December (Mobile)

1993

THE GAME OF LOVE AND
CHANCE
by Pierre Marivaux
trans. by Neil Bartlett
Dir. Mike Alfreds & Neil Bartlett
Cottesloe 11 January
(co-production by Cambridge
Theatre Company & Gloria in
association with the National)

THE DAY AFTER
TOMORROW
by Roel Adam
trans. by Noel Clark
Dir. Anthony Clark
Cottesloe 4 February

TRELAWNY OF THE WELLS
by Arthur W. Pinero
Dir. John Caird
Olivier 18 February

MR A'S AMAZING MAZE
PLAYS
by Alan Ayckbourn
Dir. Alan Ayckbourn
Cottesloe 4 March

MACBETH
by William Shakespeare
Dir. Richard Eyre
Olivier 1 April

ARCADIA
by Tom Stoppard
Dir. Trevor Nunn
Lyttelton 13 April

SPRINGBOARDS – *WORK
FROM STUDIO THEATRES:
THE NEIGHBOUR*
by Meredith Oakes
Dir. John Burgess
Cottesloe 21 April
SOMEWHERE
by Judith Johnson
Dir. Polly Teale
Cottesloe 24 April
(Studio/Liverpool Playhouse
co-production)
HOVE devised by the Studio
and Talking Tongues
Dir. David Farr
Cottesloe 28 April
BABY DOLL chamber opera
by Andrew Poppy
from original screenplay by
Tennessee Williams
Dir. Julia Bardsley
Cottesloe 5 May
(Studio /Leicester Haymarket
co-production)
HE WHO SAW EVERYTHING
fragments from the Epic of
Gilgamesh in a verse trans.
by Robert Temple
Dir. Tim Supple
Cottesloe 12 May

ON THE LEDGE
by Alan Bleasdale
Dir. Robin Lefevre
Lyttelton 27 April
(co-production with Nottingham
Playhouse)

SWEENEY TODD
music & lyrics by
Stephen Sondheim
book by Hugh Wheeler from an
adaptation by Christopher Bond
Dir. Declan Donnellan
Cottesloe 2 June

INADMISSIBLE EVIDENCE
by John Osborne
Dir. Di Trevis
Lyttelton 17 June

THE MOUNTAIN GIANTS
by Luigi Pirandello
version by Charles Wood
Dir. William Gaskill
Cottesloe 14 July

THE ABSENCE OF WAR
by David Hare
Dir. Richard Eyre
Olivier 2 October
(presented as *THE DAVID
HARE TRILOGY* with *Racing
Demon* and *Murmuring Judges*)

JAMAIS VU
by Ken Campbell
Dir. Colin Watkeys
Cottesloe 7 October
(presented as trilogy with
Furtive Nudist and *Pigspurt*)

MACHINAL
by Sophie Treadwell
Dir. Stephen Daldry
Lyttelton 15 October

ANGELS IN AMERICA:
Part Two *Perestroika*
by Tony Kushner
Dir. Declan Donnellan
Cottesloe 20 November
(presented with Part One:
Millennium Approaches)

MOTHER COURAGE AND
HER CHILDREN
by Bertolt Brecht
version by Hanif Kureishi
with lyrics by Sue Davies
Dir. Anthony Clark
Cottesloe 6 December (Mobile)

1994

THE SKRIKER
by Caryl Churchill
Dir. Les Waters
Cottesloe 27 January

WICKED, YAAR!
by Garry Lyons
Dir. John Turner
Cottesloe 8 March (Mobile)

THE BIRTHDAY PARTY
by Harold Pinter
Dir. Sam Mendes
Lyttelton 17 March

JOHNNY ON A SPOT
by Charles MacArthur
Dir. Richard Eyre
Olivier 31 March

LES PARENTS TERRIBLES
by Jean Cocteau
trans. by Jeremy Sams
Dir. Sean Mathias
Lyttelton 21 April

PERICLES
by William Shakespeare
Dir. Phyllida Lloyd
Olivier 19 May

RUTHERFORD AND SON
by Githa Sowerby
Dir. Katie Mitchell
Cottesloe 2 June

SWEET BIRD OF YOUTH
by Tennessee Williams
Dir. Richard Eyre
Lyttelton 16 June

THE SEAGULL
by Anton Chekhov
version by Pam Gems
Dir. John Caird
Olivier 7 July

LE CID
by Pierre Corneille
trans. by Ranjit Bolt
Dir. Jonathan Kent
Cottesloe 28 July

BROKEN GLASS
by Arthur Miller
Dir. David Thacker
Lyttelton 4 August

THE DEVIL'S DISCIPLE
by Bernard Shaw
Dir. Christopher Morahan
Olivier 8 September

TWO WEEKS WITH THE
QUEEN
adapted by Mary Morris
from the novel by Morris
Gleitzman
Dir. Alan Ayckbourn
Cottesloe 20 September
(co-production with Stephen
Joseph Theatre, Scarborough)

THE CHILDREN'S HOUR
by Lillian Hellman
Dir. Howard Davies
Lyttelton 22 September

ALICE'S ADVENTURES
UNDER GROUND
by Christopher Hampton
adapted from the writings of
Lewis Carroll, in collaboration
with Martha Clarke
Dir. Martha Clarke
Cottesloe 8 November

LANDSCAPE
by Harold Pinter
Dir. Harold Pinter
Cottesloe 23 November

OUT OF A HOUSE WALKED
A MAN...
musical scenes from the writings
of Daniil Kharms
devised by Theatre de Complicite
Dir. Simon McBurney
Lyttelton 1 December
(co-production with Theatre
de Complicite)

1995

LEAVE TAKING
by Winsome Pinnock
Dir. Paulette Randall
Cottesloe 4 January (Mobile)

THE MERRY WIVES OF
WINDSOR
by William Shakespeare
Dir. Terry Hands
Olivier 26 January

DEALER'S CHOICE
by Patrick Marber
Dir. Patrick Marber
Cottesloe 9 February

WHAT THE BUTLER SAW
by Joe Orton
Dir. Phyllida Lloyd
Lyttelton 2 March

WOMEN OF TROY
by Euripides
trans. by Kenneth McLeish
Dir. Annie Castledine
Olivier 16 March

THE BLUE BALL
by Paul Godfrey
Dir. Paul Godfrey
Cottesloe 30 March

UNDER MILK WOOD
by Dylan Thomas
Dir. Roger Michell
Olivier 13 April

SKYLIGHT
by David Hare
Dir. Richard Eyre
Cottesloe 4 May

ABSOLUTE HELL
by Rodney Ackland
Dir. Anthony Page
Lyttelton 23 May

RICHARD II
by William Shakespeare
Dir. Deborah Warner
Cottesloe 2 June

1996

LA GRANDE MAGIA
by Eduardo de Filippo
trans. by Carlo Ardito
Dir. Richard Eyre
Lyttelton 13 July

TITUS ANDRONICUS
by William Shakespeare
Dir. Gregory Doran
Cottesloe 18 July
(Market Theatre Johannesburg
in association with the Studio)

VOLPONE
by Ben Jonson
Dir. Matthew Warchus
Olivier 27 July

THE MACHINE WRECKERS
by Ernst Toller
in a version by Ashley Dukes
Dir. Katie Mitchell
Cottesloe 11 August

WILD OATS
by John O'Keeffe
Dir. Jeremy Sams
Lyttelton 7 September

A LITTLE NIGHT MUSIC
music & lyrics by Stephen
Sondheim
book by Hugh Wheeler
Dir. Sean Mathias
Olivier 26 September

THE WAY OF THE WORLD
by William Congreve
Dir. Phyllida Lloyd
Lyttelton 19 October

CYRANO
by Edmond Rostand
adapted by Jatinder Verma
rendered into verse by Ranjit Bolt
Dir. Anuradha Kapur
Cottesloe 25 October
(co-production with Tara Arts)

MOTHER COURAGE AND
HER CHILDREN
by Bertolt Brecht
version by David Hare
Dir. Jonathan Kent
Olivier 14 November

ROSENCRANTZ AND
GUILDENSTERN ARE DEAD
by Tom Stoppard
Dir. Matthew Francis
Lyttelton 14 December

STANLEY
by Pam Gems
Dir. John Caird
Cottesloe 1 February

THE ENDS OF THE EARTH
by David Lan
Dir. Andrei Serban
Cottesloe 29 February

FROGS
by Aristophanes
in a musical adaptation by
Fiona Laird
Dir. Fiona Laird
Cottesloe 15 March (Mobile)

MARY STUART
by Friedrich Schiller
trans. by Jeremy Sams
Dir. Howard Davies
Lyttelton 21 March

THE PRINCE'S PLAY
by Victor Hugo (Le Roi s'amuse)
verse translation by
Tony Harrison
Dir. Richard Eyre
Olivier 19 April

THE DESIGNATED
MOURNER
by Wallace Shawn
Dir. David Hare
Cottesloe 24 April

BLUE REMEMBERED HILLS
by Dennis Potter
Dir. Patrick Marber
Lyttelton 2 May

WAR AND PEACE
adapted by Helen Edmundson
from the novel by Leo Tolstoy
Dir. Nancy Meckler & Polly
Teale
Cottesloe 25 June
(co-production with Shared
Experience)

JOHN GABRIEL BORKMAN
by Henrik Ibsen
in a new version by
Nicholas Wright
Dir. Richard Eyre
Lyttelton 11 July

Judi Dench in *A Little
Night Music*, 1995
(Photo: Mark Douet)

1997

THE RED BALLOON
by Albert Lamorisse
adapted for the stage by
Anthony Clark
with music by Mark Vibrans
Dir. Anthony Clark
Olivier 1 August

BLINDED BY THE SUN
by Stephen Poliakoff
Dir. Ron Daniels
Cottesloe 3 September

THE OEDIPUS PLAYS
Oedipus the King
and
Oedipus at Colonus
by Sophocles
trans. by Ranjit Bolt
Dir. Peter Hall
Olivier 17 September

VIOLIN TIME
by Ken Campbell
Dir. Colin Watkeys
Cottesloe 2 October

THE ALCHEMIST
by Ben Jonson
Dir. Bill Alexander
Olivier 9 October
(co-production with Birmingham
Repertory Theatre)

DEATH OF A SALESMAN
by Arthur Miller
Dir. David Thacker
Lyttelton 31 October

FAIR LADIES AT A GAME OF
POEM CARDS
verse play by Peter Oswald
based on an original work by
Chikamatsu Monzaemon
version by Frank McGuinness
Dir. John Crowley
Cottesloe 20 November

GUYS AND DOLLS
based on a story and characters
of Damon Runyon
music & lyrics by Frank Loesser
book by Jo Swerling &
Abe Burrows
Dir. Richard Eyre
Musical staging by David Toguri
Olivier 17 December

THE CRIPPLE OF
INISHMAAN
by Martin McDonagh
Dir. Nicholas Hytner
Cottesloe 7 January

LIGHT SHINING IN
BUCKINGHAMSHIRE
by Caryl Churchill
Dir. Mark Wing-Davey
Cottesloe 10 January (Mobile)

THE HOMECOMING
by Harold Pinter
Dir. Roger Michell
Lyttelton 23 January

CARDIFF EAST
by Peter Gill
Dir. Peter Gill
Cottesloe 12 February

LADY IN THE DARK
a musical play by Moss Hart
lyrics by Ira Gershwin
music by Kurt Weill
Dir. Francesca Zambello
Lyttelton 11 March

KING LEAR
by William Shakespeare
Dir. Richard Eyre
Cottesloe 27 March

THE CAUCASIAN CHALK
CIRCLE
by Bertolt Brecht
version by Frank McGuinness
Dir. Simon McBurney
Olivier in-the-round 21 April

THE PERSECUTION AND
ASSASSINATION OF MARAT
AS PERFORMED BY THE
INMATES OF THE ASYLUM
OF CHARENTON UNDER
THE DIRECTION OF THE
MARQUIS DE SADE
by Peter Weiss
English version by Geoffrey
Skelton
verse adaptation by Adrian
Mitchell
Dir. Jeremy Sams
Olivier in-the-round 14 May

TWELFTH NIGHT
by William Shakespeare
Dir: Brigid Larmour
Cottesloe 16 May (Mobile)
CLOSER
by Patrick Marber
Dir. Patrick Marber
Cottesloe 29 May

AMY'S VIEW
by David Hare
Dir. Richard Eyre
Lyttelton 20 June

CHIPS WITH EVERYTHING
by Arnold Wesker
Dir. Howard Davies
Lyttelton 4 September

OTHELLO
by William Shakespeare
Dir. Sam Mendes
Cottesloe 16 September
(co-production with Salzburg
Festival)

AN ENEMY OF THE PEOPLE
by Henrik Ibsen
version by Christopher Hampton
Dir. Trevor Nunn
Olivier 19 September

THE INVENTION OF LOVE
by Tom Stoppard
Dir. Richard Eyre
Cottesloe 1 October

111

AUDIENCE MEMORIES

1969

I came to see **The White Devil** on a day return from Bristol as background to an A-level course on Jacobean tragedy. At the time, I was keener on film than theatre, so the fact that Fellini's designer was involved meant rather more to me than the director or actors. And it's the design I still remember – the grotesque, tottering wigs, and the set that seemed to be comprised of quarried layers of rock. But at the time it was the extraordinary violence of the production that shocked (and thrilled) me. One murder was performed as a slow-motion masque, totally silent except for a sharp crack as Flamineo broke his adversary's neck.
Michael Stoteley, Bristol

1973

My earliest memory of the Old Vic is attending 1963's *Hamlet* with my aunt. The interval's lemon squash impressed me far more than the play....
In 1972 my love for theatre blossomed. Fifty-seven trips were made to the Old Vic to view Diana Rigg's Lady Macbeth, Célimène in **The Misanthrope** and Dottie in *Jumpers*. What performances!
David Cheyne, Detroit, USA

1976

The opening production in the Olivier, **Tamburlaine The Great**, was a stunning piece of

theatre in what was going to become my favourite auditorium. But the moment in it which has stayed with me ever since was when the lights turned to red, covering the whole of the circular stage, and then moved steadily out to bathe the entire audience in blood, including us all in Tamburlaine's imperial ambitions. It was both exhilarating and frightening, making us realise the complexity of identifying with a charismatic but violent character.
Helen King, East Sussex

1978

What an impression **Lark Rise** made. Eyeball to eyeball and a wrestler's shove from Brian Glover in the market scene, losing my partner to James Grant in the final country dance but above all the magic moment when the group of reapers advanced through the pit audience and harvested us – obedient, quiet, submissive to the swish of the scythes.
Brian Gatward, Essex

Ralph Richardson
in rehearsal for
The Cherry Orchard
(Photo: Zoë Dominic)

Anthony Higgins, Brian Cox,
Tom Georgeson and
Paul Moriarty in
Danton's Death
(Photo: Nobby Clark)

Susan Fleetwood and
Derek Newark in
A Midsummer Night's Dream
(Photo: Michael Mayhew)

Dave Hill and Brenda Blethyn
in *The Nativity*
(Photo: Nobby Clark)

1978
The Cherry Orchard: At the end of this remarkable play we watched Sir Ralph, as Firs, gently lowering himself down to die in the empty room. Nineteen years on and my eyes still fill with tears when I recall these wonderful moments.
Bob Snow, Isle of Wight

1982
Büchner's **Danton's Death** directed by Peter Gill (1982-3), was the most moving and thrilling production I had ever seen. During the last months of the run I had stumbled in an emotional daze from one performance to the next, missing none.
At the end of the final matinee Brian Cox [playing Danton] presented me with a bouquet in recognition of my evident enthusiasm. When I had recovered sufficiently from the shock to look up, I found that the entire cast was applauding me. I have never been so delighted – and embarrassed – in my life. I had always believed I was invisible.
Isabel Monk, London

1982
A Midsummer Night's Dream:
When we arrived at the Cottesloe, my son Ben insisted on sitting on stage although the four of us had to share the last remaining cushion... At the end when Puck said, "Give me your hands, if we be friends", we all held out our hands except my Ben who sat resolutely on his. Susan Fleetwood, now alas no longer with us, dropped the lightest of kisses on him....Ben was permanently enchanted.
Cynthia Greenwood, Berkshire

1980
We took our two rather blasé teenage children to see **The Nativity**. The time came for Mary (Brenda Blethyn) to give birth, and the smallest children in the audience were given torches to hold "to light the stable for the baby Jesus to be born". The rest of the lights were dimmed, so that all you could see were the faces of the children, holding up their torches, which they did with the *utmost* solemnity. It is the face of one little boy in particular, which provides my abiding memory of the National Theatre. He must have been about four years old – and he was truly in the presence of a miracle. He brought tears to my eyes – and even my teenagers were touched.
Gill Jefford, High Wycombe

Michael Hordern in *The Rivals*
(Photo: Zoë Dominic)

Anthony Hopkins and
Judi Dench as
Antony and Cleopatra
(Photo: John Haynes)

Antony Sher in *Arturo Ui*
(Photo: Clive Barda)

Emma Fielding and
Rufus Sewell in *Arcadia*
(Photo: Richard Mildenhall)

Fiona Shaw in *Machinal* (Photo:
Ivan Kyncl)

1983

The Olivier Theatre, 12 October 1983. Michael Hordern played Sir Anthony Absolute in Sheridan's **The Rivals**. His cracking open and eating a boiled egg while apoplectic with rage was one of the funniest pieces of "stage business" ever. At curtain call, the audience cheered for many minutes. Then Sir Michael stepped forward and held up his hand for silence. He told us that Ralph Richardson had died earlier that day. Everyone was still, and then we all filed out slowly in silence.
The Revd. Peter Beech, Essex

1987

Antony and Cleopatra: The magic of acting: Judi Dench as Cleopatra in 1987 was so bewitching, shimmering as much as her costume, that the tragedy came to life for me for the first time.
Susan Morgans, Berkhamsted

1993

Arcadia is magic. Certainly, the performance I saw was. Everything was perfect – that beautiful set, the dialogue, the incredibly perfect casting – everything came together and totally entranced me. By the end of the play, I was speechless with joy, with the "rightness" of the whole production. I can't recall any other play affecting me in such a way.
Diana B Dorken, Philadelphia, USA

1991

The Resistible Rise of Arturo Ui: The play was marvellous; Antony Sher, stunning. That day changed my theatre-going. I now see as many and as varied productions as I have money and time for. I still join the noon queue for a standby and then enjoy all else that the National has to offer.
Elizabeth Turner, Kent

1993

Machinal: For me, Fiona Shaw's performance put her amongst the greatest of actresses. I am still haunted by her progression to the electric chair.
Bruce Thompson, London

Desmond Barrit in
The Mountain Giants
(Photo: John Haynes)

Alan Howard in
La Grande Magia
(Photo: John Haynes)

Paul Scofield and
Vanessa Redgrave in
JohnGabriel Borkman
(Photo: John Haynes)

1995
Opera never meant much to me. But that changed dramatically when I saw Alan Howard as Calogero di Spelta in **La Grande Magia**. I saw the play three times and each time I particularly enjoyed the moment when he sang an aria... Only afterwards and by chance I found out that it is Cavaradossi's aria from *Tosca*. I have seen *Tosca* five times since then and have been to other operas (not only Puccini) as well, greatly enjoying them.
Kerstin Schröder, Hamburg, Germany

1993
The production of which I'd practically sponsor a revival single-handed is one that barely got noticed, of a baffling play, that survived a bare month or two in the Cottesloe. **The Mountain Giants**... the whole play has lingered in my mind longer than any of the countless others we've seen.
Piers Burton-Page, London

1996
John Gabriel Borkman in late 1996...one of my theatrical highlights of the decade, even bringing me whooping and cheering to my feet for the curtain call, which being British I don't like to do too often.
David Burt, Brighton

VISITS TO THE NATIONAL

1964

Bristol Old Vic Company
LOVE'S LABOUR'S LOST
by William Shakespeare
Dir. Val May
Old Vic 7 September

HENRY V
by William Shakespeare
Dir. Stuart Burge
Old Vic 11 September

Proclemer-Albertazzi Company
HAMLET
by William Shakespeare
trans. by Gerardo Guerrieri
Dir. Franco Zeffirelli
Old Vic 15 September

1965

Berliner Ensemble
THE RESISTIBLE RISE OF
ARTURO UI
by Bertolt Brecht
Dir. Manfred Wekwerth/
Peter Palitzsch
Old Vic 9 August

CORIOLANUS
by William Shakespeare/
Bertolt Brecht
Dir. Manfred Wekwerth/
Joachim Tenschert
Old Vic 10 August

THE THREEPENNY OPERA
by Bertolt Brecht
Dir. Erich Engel
Old Vic 11 August

THE DAYS OF THE
COMMUNE
by Bertolt Brecht
Dir. Manfred Wekwerth/
Joachim Tenschert
Old Vic 12 August

National Youth Theatre
ANTONY AND CLEOPATRA
by William Shakespeare
Dir. Michael Croft
Old Vic 6 September
TROILUS AND CRESSIDA
by William Shakespeare
Dir. Paul Hill
Old Vic 13 September

Le Théâtre du Nouveau Monde
L'ECOLE DES FEMMES
by Molière
Dir. Jean Gascon
Old Vic 20 September

KLONDYKE
by Jacques Languirand &
Gabriel Charpentier
Dir. Jean Gascon
Old Vic 23 September

1969

Compagnie Renaud-Barrault
RABELAIS
by Jean-Louis Barrault
based on Rabelais
Dir. Jean-Louis Barrault
Old Vic 24 September

1970

Nottingham Playhouse Company
THE ALCHEMIST
by Ben Jonson
Dir. Stuart Burge
Old Vic 9 February

KING LEAR
by William Shakespeare
Dir. Jonathan Miller
Old Vic 10 February

Abbey Theatre Company
THE DANDY DOLLS
by George Fitzmaurice
Dir. Hugh Hunt
and
THE WELL OF THE SAINTS
by J M Synge
Dir. Hugh Hunt
Old Vic 3 August

Nottingham Playhouse Company
A YARD OF SUN
by Christopher Fry
Dir. Stuart Burge
Old Vic 10 August

1971

Bolton Octagon Theatre Company
THE FATHER
by August Strindberg
Trans. Michael Meyer
Dir. Geoffrey Ost
Old Vic 24 August

Theatre Royal York Company
THE LAST SWEET DAYS
OF ISAAC
Book & Lyrics by Gretchen Cryer
Music by Nancy Ford
Dir. Donald Bodley
Old Vic 6 September

Belgian National Theatre Company
PANTAGLEIZE
by Michel de Ghelderode
Dir. Frank Dunlop
Old Vic 16 September

THE SEVENTH
COMMANDMENT
by Dario Fo
Trans. by Sandra Camasio
Dir. Arturo Corso (based on
conception by Dario Fo)
Old Vic 17 September

1975

Nottingham Playhouse Company
COMEDIANS
by Trevor Griffiths
Dir. Richard Eyre
Old Vic 24 September

1976

Théâtre National Populaire
TARTUFFE
by Moliere
Dir. Roger Planchon
Lyttelton 17 November

LA DISPUTE
by Marivaux
Dir. Patrice Chéreau
Lyttelton 23 November

1977

Schaubühne am Halleschen Üfer
SUMMERFOLK
by Maxim Gorki
adapted by Peter Stein and
Botho Strauss
Dir. Peter Stein
Lyttelton 3 March

Science Fiction Theatre of Liverpool
ILLUMINATUS
by Ken Campbell & Chris
Langham
from books by Robert Shea and
Robert Anton Wilson
Dir. Ken Campbell & Chris
Langham
Cottesloe 4 March

Phoenix Theatre, Leicester
THE MAGIC DRUM
by James Kirkup, adapted by
Michael Bogdanov
Dir. Michael Bogdanov
Lyttelton 29 March

*Birmingham Repertory Theatre
Company*
THE DEVIL IS AN ASS
by Ben Jonson
adapted by Peter Barnes
Dir. Stuart Burge
Lyttelton 2 May

MEASURE FOR MEASURE
by William Shakespeare
Dir. Stuart Burge
Lyttelton 5 May

*Manchester Library Theatre
Company*
SELL-OUT
by Roger Smith &
Tom Kempinski
Dir. David Scase
Cottesloe 9 May

Nuria Espert Company
DIVINAS PALABRAS
by Don Ramón Maria del
Valle Inclan
Dir. Victor Garcia
Lyttelton 14 June

Chris Harris
KEMP'S JIG
Compiled by Chris Harris &
John David
Dir. John David
Cottesloe 11 July

London Theatre Group
EAST
by Steven Berkoff
Dir. Steven Berkoff
Cottesloe 19 July

METAMORPHOSIS
by Franz Kafka
adapted by Steven Berkoff
Dir. Steven Berkoff
Cottesloe 29 July

English Stage Company
FOR THE WEST
by Michael Hastings
Dir. Nicholas Wright
Cottesloe 15 August

*Glyndebourne Festival Opera
with the LPO*
DON GIOVANNI
by Mozart
Dir. Peter Hall
Lyttelton 16 August

London Theatre Group
THE FALL OF THE HOUSE
OF USHER
by Edgar Allen Poe
adapted by Steven Berkoff &
Terry James
Dir. Steven Berkoff
Cottesloe 1 November

Moving Being
BABEL'S DANCER
conceived by Geoff Moore
Dir. Geoff Moore
Cottesloe 22 November

Paine's Plough Company
RICHARD III PART 2
by David Pownall
Dir. Edward Adams
Cottesloe 5 December

MOTOCAR
by David Pownall
Dir. Edward Adams
Cottesloe 6 December

1980

Market Theatre, Johannesburg
A LESSON FROM ALOES
by Athol Fugard
Dir. Athol Fugard
Cottesloe 10 July

1983

Market Theatre, Johannesburg
MASTER HAROLD...AND
THE BOYS
by Athol Fugard
Dir. Athol Fugard
Cottesloe 24 November

1984

Glyndebourne Opera
WHERE THE WILD THINGS
ARE
by Oliver Knussen
libretto by Maurice Sendak
Conductors Oliver Knussen/
Jane Glover
Dir. Frank Corsaro
Lyttelton 9 January

1987

*Market Theatre, Johannesburg
present The Earth Players*
BOPHA!
by Percy Mtwa
Dir. Percy Mtwa
Cottesloe 8 January

Schaubühne Company, West Berlin
THE HAIRY APE
by Eugene O'Neill
German trans. by Peter Stein
Dir. Peter Stein
Lyttelton 11 May

Royal Dramatic Theatre, Stockholm
HAMLET
by William Shakespeare
Swedish trans. by
Britt G Hallqvist
Dir. Ingmar Bergman
Lyttelton 10 June

MISS JULIE
by August Strindberg
Dir. Ingmar Bergman
Lyttelton 17 June

Manchester Library Theatre
EFFIE'S BURNING
by Valerie Winsor
Dir. Susan Mayo
Cottesloe 29 June

Ninagawa Company, Tokyo
MACBETH
by William Shakespeare
trans. by Yushi Odajima
Dir. Yukio Ninagawa
Lyttelton 17 September

MEDEA
by Euripides
scenario by Mutsuo Takahashi
Dir. Yukio Ninagawa
Olivier 24 September

Mayakovsky Theatre Company
TOMORROW WAS WAR
by Boris Vassiliev
Dir. A A Goncharov
Lyttelton 28 October

1988

Field Day Theatre Company
MAKING HISTORY
by Brian Friel
Dir. Simon Curtis
Cottesloe 5 December

1989

Teatro del Sur, Buenos Aires
TANGO VARSOVIANA
by Alberto Felix Alberto
Dir. Alberto Felix Alberto
Cottesloe 24 May

Steppenwolf Theatre Company,
Chicago
THE GRAPES OF WRATH
by John Steinbeck
adapted by Frank Galati
Dir. Frank Galati
Lyttelton 22 June

Moscow Art Theatre
UNCLE VANYA
by Anton Chekhov
Dir. Oleg Yefremov
Lyttelton 14 September

Ninagawa Company, Tokyo
SUICIDE FOR LOVE
based on Chikamatsu
Monzaemon
by Matsuyo Akimoto
Dir. Yukio Ninagawa
Lyttelton 9 October

1990

Shared Experience/Soho Theatre
Company
ABINGDON SQUARE
by Maria Irene Fornes
Dir. Nancy Meckler
Cottesloe 29 March

Market Theatre Company,
Johannesburg
MY CHILDREN, MY AFRICA
by Athol Fugard
Dir. Athol Fugard
Lyttelton 6 September

Bulandra Theatre, Romania
HAMLET
by William Shakespeare
Trans. by Nina Cassian
Dir. Alexandru Tocilescu
Lyttelton 20 September

Abbey Theatre, Dublin
DANCING AT LUGHNASA
by Brian Friel
Dir. Patrick Mason
Lyttelton 15 October

Contemporary Legend Theatre
Company, Taiwan
THE KINGDOM OF DESIRE
by Lee Hue-min from
Shakespeare's Macbeth
Dir. Wu Sing-Kuo
Lyttelton 14 November

Théâtre Repère, Québec
TECTONIC PLATES
by Robert Lepage and
Théâtre Repère
Dir. Robert Lepage
Cottesloe 6 December

1991

Theatre de Complicite
THE VISIT
by Friedrich Dürrenmatt
adapt. by Maurice Valency
Dir. Annabel Arden with Simon
McBurney
Lyttelton 13 February

Schochiku Company, Japan
GRAND KABUKI
Lyttelton 4 October

1992

Robert Lepage
NEEDLES AND OPIUM
solo piece by Robert Lepage
Dir. Robert Lepage
(Presented in association with
Cultural Industry Ltd.)
Cottesloe 30 April

Piccolo Teatro, Milan
LE BARUFFE CHIOZZOTTE
by Carlo Goldoni
Dir. Giorgio Strehler
Lyttelton 28 October

Franco Zeffirelli Company, Rome
SEI PERSONAGGI IN CERCA
D'AUTORE
by Luigi Pirandello
new version by Franco Zeffirelli
& Luigi Vanzi
Dir. Franco Zeffirelli
Lyttelton 9 November

1994

Peter Brook Company, Paris
THE MAN WHO
inspired by the book by
Oliver Sacks
Dir. Peter Brook
Cottesloe 5 May

1996

Ex Machina
THE SEVEN STREAMS OF
THE RIVER OTA
conceived by Robert Lepage &
Ex Machina
Dir. Robert Lepage
Lyttelton 21 September

1997

Robert Lepage
ELSINORE
a solo work by Robert Lepage
based on Shakespeare's Hamlet
Lyttelton 4 January

Comédie Française
LES FAUSSES
CONFIDENCES
by Marivaux
Dir. Jean-Pierre Miquel
Lyttelton 30 September

INDEX
of persons and play titles